$PROUT!

$PROUT!

Everything I Need
to Know about
Sales
I Learned from
My Garden

Alan Vengel & Greg Wright

BK

BERRETT-KOEHLER PUBLISHERS, INC.
San Francisco

Berrett-Koehler Publishers, Inc.
235 Montgomery Street, Suite 650
San Francisco, CA 94104-2916
Tel: (415) 288-0260   Fax: (415) 362-2512   www.bkconnection.com

ORDERING INFORMATION
Quantity sales. Special discounts are available on quantity purchases by corporations, associations, and others. For details, contact the "Special Sales Department" at the Berrett-Koehler address above.
Individual sales. Berrett-Koehler publications are available through most bookstores. They can also be ordered direct from Berrett-Koehler: Tel: (800) 929-2929; Fax: (802) 864-7626; www.bkconnection.com
Orders for college textbook/course adoption use. Please contact Berrett-Koehler: Tel: (800) 929-2929; Fax: (802) 864-7626.
Orders by U.S. trade bookstores and wholesalers. Please contact Publishers Group West, 1700 Fourth Street, Berkeley, CA 94710. Tel: (510) 528-1444; Fax (510) 528-3444.

Berrett-Koehler and the BK logo are registered trademarks of Berrett-Koehler Publishers, Inc.

Printed in the United States of America

Berrett-Koehler books are printed on long-lasting acid-free paper. When it is available, we choose paper that has been manufactured by environmentally responsible processes. These may include using trees grown in sustainable forests, incorporating recycled paper, minimizing chlorine in bleaching, or recycling the energy produced at the paper mill.

Library of Congress Catloging-in-Publication Data
Vengel, Alan, 1947 –
    SPROUT! Everything I needed to know about sales I learned from my garden: four steps to sales success / Alan Vnegel & Greg Wright.
        p.cm.
    ISBN 1-57675-207-0
        1. Selling.   I. Wright, Greg, 1949- II. Title
HF5438.25.V46 2003
658.85—dc22   2003060776

First Edition
08 07 06 05 04 03   10 9 8 7 6 5 4 3 2 1

Designer: Dianne Platner
Copyeditor: Elissa Rabellino
Illustrations: Copyright © 2004 by Iskra Johnson

Contents

Preface

sprout, vb.: to spring up; to send out new growth

Why a book relating sales success to gardening?

Because we believe that there is more than one way to look at the challenge of getting the most out of your sales career. Our book offers a new way of looking at sales that you're not likely to have encountered.

We have had the privilege of building sales careers that have been fun as well as profitable. We've also enjoyed working with thousands of successful salespeople in all different stages of their careers, and we've learned a lot from them in the process. Through the sales professionals we've met, we've become aware of the importance of two themes in particular: the stages of career satisfaction, or happiness, with what they have accomplished; and their level of optimism about their future.

Specifically, we've noticed distinct plateaus in the

energy of the salespeople with whom we have worked. Although all career choices present challenges for sustaining success, it is evident to us that sales professionals in particular are constantly measured against rigid, economically driven barometers and exposed to constant internal and external competition.

Consequently, feelings of frustration and harmful stress run very high in the sales industry. The cost to sales organizations in lost talent, rehiring, and retraining hurts the corporate bottom line. Unfortunately, the emotional toll of high stress can be devastating to any sales professional's career.

In our experience, sales professionals don't always acknowledge that pressure. Or if they do, they internalize it. That's a big mistake. While most salespeople are well schooled in the nuts and bolts of the selling process, the feeling that there seems to be something missing can cause a loss of optimism and premature burnout.

That's where SPROUT! comes in handy. We have found that using a metaphor we call the Sales Garden and its accompanying mind-set can help relieve some harmful stress and put more fun and passion into the selling process.

By absorbing our simple Sales Garden concept and following the user-friendly steps outlined in this book, salespeople can beat the career blues and sustain themselves for the long term, regaining their passion for sales in the process. But that's not all. Our simple formula also enables organizations to better retain precious talent by applying a philosophy that supports their sales professionals throughout the inevitable ups and downs that mark a selling career— and that creates a healthy sales framework as well.

All this from seeds sowed in our Sales Garden.

From Alan Vengel

A brief note of gratitude to some of the people who have helped me grow during this fun project: Kathleen, my wife; David, my son; Judy, my business partner; Carol and Shawn at Vengel Lash Associates; Steven Piersanti, Jeevan Sivasubramaniam, Kristen Frantz, Michael Crowley, María Jesús Aguiló, and the rest of the gang at Berrett-Koehler, with special thanks to Brenda Frink, who came up with the title

for this book; Vicki Webster, our gardening consultant; Elissa Rabellino, our copyeditor; and Beverly
Kaye. Thank you all for encouraging me to SPROUT!

From Greg Wright

My thanks to all the sales professionals I have had
the privilege to work with over the past thirty years.
Their candor in relating their experiences, and their
openness to developing new selling skills, have given
me the "seeds" that grew into this book.

Alan Vengel and Greg Wright
December 2003

Chapter One

The Sales Garden

Tired.

Flat-out, bone-weary tired.

That's how Marsha Molloy was feeling, eight years into a sales career that was losing steam fast.

A successful medical-supply sales representative whose nickname in her salad days was "Marsha Money," she had hit hard times, laid low by a tough economy and a declining interest in the profession she had embraced since starting out as a catalog sales rep right out of high school. The once-hungry top producer had seemingly lost her touch and grown indifferent to a sales culture that appeared to value faxes, e-mails, and cell phone chats instead of the relationship building that had been her forte. Worse, she'd lost her passion for the sales business and forgotten the reasons why she'd entered the business in the first place: the face-to-face interaction, the thrill of closing a deal, the satisfaction of building long-term relationships.

It was a strange feeling for someone who had always felt at home in the sales world, Marsha thought.

After all, she had the classic sales background, didn't she? She had started in grade school, selling candies door-to-door, buying them for a quarter and selling them for 50 cents to kids who had allowance money that was burning a hole in their pockets. She became more involved in sales in high school, where she took a part-time job after school selling baby pictures to proud parents—especially mothers—in her town. She learned, through trial and error, that she could package the pictures in such a way that people usually purchased the set she wanted them to buy. By asking a proud mom whether she wanted the bargain package or the value package, she found that the mom would usually opt for the more expensive value package. Nobody wanted to skimp on her baby pictures, and Marsha learned that people buy on emotions.

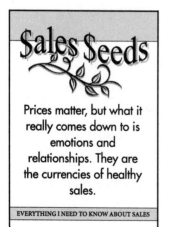

Sales Seeds

Prices matter, but what it really comes down to is emotions and relationships. They are the currencies of healthy sales.

EVERYTHING I NEED TO KNOW ABOUT SALES

She dabbled in sales all through college, selling tie-dyed shirts to fellow students on the campus concourse at the University of Massachusetts and later marketing "Florida Break" spring vacations for a local travel agent, who gave Marsha 50 percent of the cut for bringing her the business.

After college she went right to work selling ad time for a big-city radio station and later switched to medical-supply sales when a key customer moved to that field and made her an offer she couldn't refuse. There she learned the art of sales—the importance of developing a network of contacts that could, like her travel agent boss, bring her business. She learned how to keep herself sharp with cold calls, but cold calls proved inefficient compared with building a network of trusted customers over time. She trained herself to focus on developing healthy, long-lasting customer relationships. After all, those accounts made up 85 percent of her sales. Marsha found that even in tough times when customers were buying less, it was the sales representative with the best contacts and the best relationships—and not the quick-hit artist—who survived and thrived.

Before long, Marsha had forged for herself a six-figure annual income, was taking plenty of trips to exotic ports of call for exceeding her quotas, and even found time to have a reasonable home and social life. For the next several years, she was on cloud nine.

But that was then and this is now, she thought. Fatigue, restlessness, and a vague sense of unhappiness had slowly enveloped her in recent months. She'd tried to talk to her husband, and then her boss, about her fatigue. She told both that she was burned out: she dreaded going to work in the morning, and making her calls and traveling through her territory—a weekly practice she'd always found enjoyable—now felt like drudgery. She had even begun feeling cynical about her boss and her company, something she dared not tell anybody. Boxed in, Marsha started to feel as if there was no hope—that she was in it for the money and couldn't make nearly as much doing anything else.

Frustrated and confused,

Sales Seeds

You can't sell when you're tired, frustrated, depressed, or unhappy. You've got to make a change.

EVERYTHING I NEED TO KNOW ABOUT SALES

Marsha thought about her future as she drove to her favorite garden store on a brisk Saturday morning in early April. A gardening buff on weekends, Marsha couldn't wait to pick out some seeds, buy some new gloves, and get back to the small patch of land behind her house, where every spring she'd planted something different. Working in her garden calmed her and gave her peace of mind—and she missed it during those barren wintry months when she couldn't get out there. Driving up the road to the nursery, tires crunching on the gravel, Marsha forgot about her career woes for the moment and headed into the parking lot.

Gently maneuvering her old Ford pickup truck into a space, she noticed something odd. Instead of "Wayland Nurseries," the sign out front read in bold blue letters, "Rawlings Garden Supply."

Confused and a tad agitated that her favorite nursery had apparently changed hands, Marsha stepped out of the truck and jogged up the cobblestone walk to the entrance in her brand-new Reeboks, an impulse purchase she'd made earlier in the week to brighten her mood. It hadn't.

She opened the door and stepped inside.

She immediately noticed that the store had changed. Instead of narrow paths between cluttered rows of seed racks, pots, plants, and garden utensils, there were wide aisles on a shiny hardwood floor. The walls had been knocked down and replaced with huge picture windows that gave the refurbished store a calm aura. Huge shafts of sunlight streamed into the store, bathing the room in warm, golden tones. Marsha didn't know who the new proprietor was, but she was impressed by what he—or she—had done to the place.

"Can I help you, Miss?"

Marsha turned around to see a tall, affable-looking man with a head of closely cropped silver hair and a bronzed, weathered face. He leaned over the counter, absentmindedly brushing some dust off the cash register.

"Mmm, yes," Marsha answered. "Planting time, you know. Going to need some seeds, some compost, and maybe a new trowel. That time of year again." She paused, fidgeting a bit. "Mind if I ask you a question?"

The man suppressed a grin. "You want to know

who this newcomer is who's running your favorite garden shop—am I right?"

Marsha relaxed a bit. "Well, I was kind of wondering."

The man extended a big, strong hand. "The name's Rawlings. Bob Rawlings. Three years retired from Pharson International. Been a salesman my whole life. Been a gardener my whole life, too—just like you, I bet. When Wayland Nurseries' owners put the place up for sale, I grabbed it. It's always been a dream of mine to run my own garden shop. And now … here I am."

Marsha shook his hand. "Marsha Molloy—a pleasure to meet you. Sales, you say?"

"Yep," replied Rawlings. "Thirty-five years in medical supplies. Lots of ups and downs, but mostly ups. I still do a little consulting on the side for the company, but only about three or four days a quarter. You know—working the shows and seminars, things like that."

Almost immediately, Marsha felt more relaxed in Rawlings' presence. Funny that he had been in sales—medical sales, no less—and loved gardening, too, she thought. "Yes, I know the drill," she said, looking over the brightly lit racks containing packets of rutabaga, carrot, and other seeds along the first aisle. "But thirty-five years, though—didn't you ever get tired of it, Mr. Rawlings? I've been in sales for eight years and I'm getting sick and tired of it already."

"Call me 'Gardener.' All my friends do," he said.

"OK, Gardener," Marsha replied. She looked around the store to see if anyone else was there. The place was empty. "But … if you don't mind my asking, did you ever lose interest in your career? You know, did you feel burned out a bit from all the pressures and deadlines and quotas?"

"Yeah, sure," Gardener replied, chuckling to himself. Boy, had he ever.

Yes, he was a former sales professional. In fact, in opening his garden store he was able to combine his two favorite passions, sales and gardening. It was no coincidence that Rawlings (whose nickname during his career had been "The Gardener" because of his penchant for comparing sales to gardening) was able to merge the characteristics of a good gardener— patience, the ability to nurture, and good timing—

into his sales career.

But he'd seen plenty of tough times. Gardener recalled a period twenty years earlier when the grass had looked a whole lot greener everywhere else but inside his sales territory. His customer list was shrinking, phone calls were going unreturned, and his career was in the doldrums. But he discovered what he considered to be a well-kept secret in the trade that few had figured out. Tending his tomato patch on summer mornings, Gardener reflected on how the process of producing his beloved vegetables was a lot like his sales career. You planted seeds, nurtured their growth, and protected them from the elements. In turn, you received a big reward come harvest time. A simple theory, yes, but a practical and highly effective one, too, he'd found. Once he began treating his business like his garden, he found, the better his business grew and the simpler his life became—and a happier, more relaxed salesman appeared. Using a gardening philosophy based on a four-step model he developed, Gardener fought his way out of his sales slump and learned a few things in the process.

Gardener moved around the counter to readjust

Sales Seeds

Envision your sales career as a garden—tend it, water it, and enjoy it, and you will reap the fruits of your labor.

EVERYTHING I NEED TO KNOW ABOUT SALES

some compost bags that had keeled over. "You know, Ms. Molloy, I remember a few times when I thought I wanted to chuck the whole thing and do something entirely different. But luxuries like food and shelter forced me to deal with my growing disinterest, for lack of a better term, in sales and in my career. I'd wager that you might be feeling some of the same, ah, pressures that I did. Am I right?"

"Yeah, some of that applies to me." She had to laugh at the unstated irony—hard to turn your back on food and shelter, she thought. Marsha also noticed that Gardener had a deep, soothing voice, like that of a late-night FM talk show host. It put her further at ease. "You don't mind my prying, do you?" Marsha asked. "My husband always teases me about my poking my nose into things. I don't want to be a bother."

Gardener laughed. "Heck, no. A fellow sales pro—and a gardening buff—in my store? That's a treat for me," he said.

Taking a deep breath, Marsha decided to open up to her new friend. She saw something in Gardener that said he liked helping people. Besides, the way things had been going lately, what did she have to lose?

She began telling Gardener her story. Her dissatisfaction with her job and her career hadn't happened overnight, Marsha began. If she could point to one thing, it may have been losing a big equipment purchase at one of her top accounts. She had thought she had it sewn up because of her ongoing relationship with one of the key decision makers. Unfortunately, someone higher up in the organization had intervened and given the deal—worth a very healthy commission—to one of her least favorite competitors. Since the economy had gone pretty flat, causing her company to make changes in her territory and commission structure, Marsha found herself thinking about getting out of the business, away from the rat race; maybe she'd start doing something fun, like running a garden shop similar to Gardener's.

At no point, Marsha told Gardener, had she felt depressed or anything like that. But the sense that she was at or near the end of her rope, careerwise, was strong. Mostly she kept her feelings to herself, but once in a while she let something slip to her husband or to a trusted coworker about how hard the business had gotten for her. About how difficult it was to get motivated to pick up the phone and cut another deal. She was tired, physically and emotionally. She knew that sooner or later her managers and customers would pick up on it. Above all, a sense of resignation had settled down over her like a fog. Dispirited, she was at a loss as to what to do about it. All Marsha knew was that something would have to give—and soon.

"Why do you suppose you're so anxious and frustrated?" Gardener asked.

Marsha immediately thought about her sense of loneliness. "I feel like I'm on an island by myself," she said. "Don't get me wrong—my husband is wonderful. But he's not in sales and really doesn't understand the pressures of the sales profession—the quotas, the deadlines, the rejection." Immediately, she felt better for having simply told someone what was bothering her.

"Looks to me that you could use some help," Gardener said. "And I hope I'm not being too forward in saying so."

Marsha sighed. "I don't know, it just seems like everything is such a drag these days. I'm just going through the motions."

Gardener nodded. He knew exactly what she meant. "Tell me, Marsha, what was it like when you were doing really well?"

"Wow, those were some good times," she answered. "I was psyched to go to work every morning … the days flew by … every call was an adventure, even the tough ones. I really liked the challenge of solving the tough customer problems, doing little things for my accounts. I came home exhausted but happy."

Gardener laughed. "Sounds like you were having F-U-N?"

"Well, yeah, I guess so," she said reflectively. "I didn't think about it that way at the time; I was so focused on the quotas and sales contests and my commission checks. But you're right—I was having a blast!"

"And you're saying it's definitely not fun for you anymore?"

Marsha realized that his remark was on target. "Yeah, somewhere along the way I lost the passion for sales ... lost the fun."

Gardener ran his fingers through his short shock of hair. "Well, one thing's for sure—you have to get the fun back in, or get out."

Marsha grimaced. "Hmmm. That seems a bit extreme; the money's still better than I can make anywhere else. And as you said, little luxuries like food and shelter, right?"

Gardener chuckled. "Yep, well, we can chat some more about that. But first, let me ask you something. Would you be here today if you didn't find gardening to be fun?"

"Hmmm, point well taken!"

Gardener continued. "Good. But the first thing you have to do is not blame yourself," he said, dusting off his hands with a clean towel now that the bags of compost were back in their rightful place. "You've got to realize that this burnout crisis of yours is a turning point, above all else. You didn't see it coming—none of us ever do—so you didn't have a plan to deal with it. But that doesn't mean you shouldn't come up with a plan. A plan is your ticket out, back to a healthy level of happiness."

Marsha thought about that. "It's funny you should mention the turning-point thing. I didn't see it coming. But then again, I've always been very proactive about handling change. Except for now. It's like I should have seen this coming but I didn't, you know?"

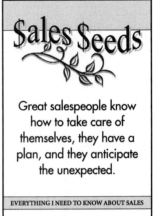

Sales Seeds

Great salespeople know how to take care of themselves, they have a plan, and they anticipate the unexpected.

EVERYTHING I NEED TO KNOW ABOUT SALES

The door opened and another customer walked into the shop. After cheerfully pointing the customer toward the garden-tools aisle, Gardener turned back to Marsha. "Careers are cyclical," he said. "Things go well for a while, and we like the direction our careers are taking us. We think that's always going to be the case. But then something happens—and it has a trigger effect that can lead you into a downward spiral. It can be problems with a boss, or the loss of a big customer. Or, on the home front, it could be problems with your marriage or with the loss of a loved one. On their own, such problems can be managed over time.

But if a domino effect kicks in and one problem leads to another, it's difficult to maintain your balance. Sooner or later, things start getting the better of you and your defense mechanisms break down. Before you know it, you think the world is conspiring against you or that you're no good at what you do anymore. And for a salesperson, self-doubt can be a real career-killer."

Marsha nodded. "I think I see what you mean," she said. "So when we hit one of these turning points, we sense that we're losing control of who we are and who we want to be. We've lost our ability to grow and to flourish."

"Exactly." Gardener replied. "It's like a garden, when you think about it. We plant a seed, nurture the plant, and harvest when the time is right. But if a calamity occurs, like a drought or a particularly rough storm, we lose control over the plant's ability to grow. Its destiny is out of our control, isn't it?"

"Yes," Marsha answered. "And the strange thing is, when you're feeling down, you think you'll always feel that way. Or if we look into the future, we don't like what we see. Just like when you plant some fruits or vegetables and a storm or a drought hits. You know you're not going to like the outcome."

She thought on that a bit as the other customer in the store hauled a few bags of potting soil and a shovel to the counter. She waited until after he left before continuing. "But even if that's the case, why am I so down about this? I just can't seem to get myself pumped up anymore."

"Well, now we're getting into deeper waters," Gardener said. "But I suspect the answer lies in the gardening analogy we were talking about, and maybe in not being so alone, trying to fight this by yourself." He sidled over to the seed section and took a few packets off the rack. "I've got an idea," he said. "If you're up for it, I think I can show you how to put your career back on track by treating your sales career like you would your own garden. We can go week to week, through the planting season all the way to harvesting. Along the way I can tell you what I've learned about tending a sales garden, so to speak, and how well it worked out for me. I've been fortunate enough to help some other people with problems similar to yours since I retired. These folks come in on Saturdays, too—we call it the 'Saturday Morning Sales Club.' All of them are in sales, and all have suffered from the low-energy burnout thing you're experiencing. Maybe we can all help you out. Interested?"

Marsha chewed her lower lip in thought. "I admit, it sounds great, but why help me? You don't even know me."

"Well, I didn't know you twenty minutes ago, that's true," Gardener answered. "But I know you better now. Besides, it wouldn't be very gentlemanly of me—or good business—not to take the time to help out a new customer. And maybe it's time for you to sprout—you know, grow in some new ways. So bring yourself around next Saturday, 9 a.m. or so, and we'll start right in."

He took the packets of seed and placed them on the counter.

Surprised, Marsha noticed that the seeds—lettuce, carrots, and radishes—were exactly what she wanted to plant. "Now how did you know what seeds I was looking to buy?" she asked.

"In all modesty," he replied, "they don't call me Gardener for nothing."

Marsha Molloy laughed, much deeper than she had in some time. "OK," she said. "See you next Saturday."

Gardening Time

The Next Morning

Gardening time can happen anywhere. It is a state of mind when one reflects on present events and plans for the future.

It was 7 a.m. on Sunday, and Marsha was up and hitting it with her new garden supplies. "Wow, this is such a great feeling," she thought. "I love this time of year … still a chill in the air, but so much promise!" She had tilled and readied the soil in her garden, and now it was time for her to begin planting the seeds she had bought the day before at Rawlings. The garden plan was all laid out, so now came the fun part—getting down into the dirt! "If only I felt this excited about going to see customers every day … "

The thought stopped her in her tracks. Hadn't

she had that kind of excitement about her sales career just a couple of years ago? And wasn't this sense of energy exactly what she and Rawlings were talking about yesterday?

As she began to sow her seeds, she laughed out loud. Treating your business as you do your garden? That was a weird way to look at things … but it seemed to work for Rawlings. He still had more energy and passion for what he did than most of her counterparts.

Her natural inclination was to take all this with a grain of salt, but it surely seemed to work for Gardener—he had a long, successful career at Johnson & Johnson, and now he was living his dream, spending all his time helping folks grow better gardens. Plus, she'd be meeting some new people, hearing about their experiences … maybe talking with these people would be fun. "Well," she thought, "let's go down next Saturday and see what unfolds." ❧

The Sales Garden Model

Planning

  🌱 Personal vision
  🌱 Set up a support group

Harvesting
🌱 Timing
🌱 Investing in renewal

Seeding

  🌱 Persistence
  🌱 Connected relationships

Nurturing
🌱 Conscious caring
🌱 Doing the right thing

Chapter Two

Planning a Sales Garden

The week passed without Marsha feeling any boost in energy. But as she got ready for her trip down to Rawlings Garden Supply to meet Gardener, she noted that things hadn't grown worse, either.

"I'll take my victories wherever I can get them," she said to herself, reaching for her keys and heading out the door.

First stop was for coffee, and then straight to the garden store. At 8:55 she strode in, sipping some hazelnut-blend coffee with one hand and carrying a bag containing doughnuts and another cup of coffee in the other.

She spied Gardener with a customer, showing her a variety of garden hoses and sprinklers. The customer peppered Gardener with questions, but Marsha noticed that he answered each one patiently, with a friendly smile. The woman laughed in a delightful "Oh right, I should have thought of it that way" manner as Gardener walked her to the register with a spray nozzle and a new sprinkler head. She paid for her purchases, and Gardener smiled and waved at her as she gathered up her goods and walked out of the store.

"People," he mused. "They never plan things out. They never have a vision." Gardener glanced over at Marsha. "Why do you suppose that is?"

"I think they're afraid to; it means they might have to think big, and people don't want to do that— sometimes they want someone to do the big picture for them," Marsha answered, handing Gardener the bag. "Careful," she said, "there's hot coffee inside."

He deftly took out the coffee and placed it on the counter. "There's something to that," he said, blowing gently on it before taking a sip. "Come on, it's a beautiful morning outside. Let's take a walk out back and see some unusual new azaleas that just came in."

Outside they went and headed down a path. They walked in silence for a moment, and then Gardener spoke. "Let me ask you something. You're in sales. Ever hear much about 'planning' to sell?"

Marsha shrugged. "I don't think so. You might have mentioned something last week. But prior to that—no."

Gardener nodded. "Planning is a big, and often overlooked, component to the sales process. All it really means is to plan your personal vision for your garden and your sales career."

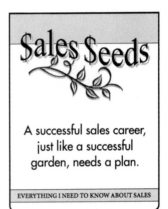

Sales Seeds

A successful sales career, just like a successful garden, needs a plan.

EVERYTHING I NEED TO KNOW ABOUT SALES

"Planning, huh? You've really thought about this gardening thing, haven't you?"

Gardener mulled over Marsha's question. "Thought about it? I lived it during the last twenty years of my sales career. In fact, I've always approached my career like a gardener approaches a patch of land," he said. "You evaluate the landscape and really examine things. You don't simply start digging where you happen to be standing."

He held up a pot of deep pink azaleas for Marsha to admire and then gently placed it back down. They walked farther down the path toward the camellias. "Like a good gardener, a salesperson should research the area for a location that's easily accessible, has good light and good soil, and is close to a water source. She shouldn't passively or carelessly adopt a sales strategy.

25

She must lay the foundation and build a blueprint for selling, just as a good gardener chooses a good location to grow his vegetables."

"She—meaning me?" asked Marsha.

"You'll do for this example," he said.

"But what does all that have to do with planning?"

"Everything," Gardener replied. "You can't have passion for something if you don't respect it, if it doesn't challenge you and make you play at the top of your game, using everything you have. I believe planning is meaningless without vision."

Marsha shook her head. "I don't know. I mean, I know I'm feeling burned out, and I recognize that I've lost my passion for sales. But 'personal vision' … I'm not sure I fully get it."

Gardener laughed. "What have you got against envisioning what your garden looks like, or what your career might look like?"

"Nothing, I guess. Honestly, I don't think about vision or planning too much. It's just a little out there for me … I've always gotten through on common sense and hard work!

Gardener grinned. "Fair enough—it's probably better that we start from scratch, anyway. That way we don't have to, ah, unlearn anything." He paused to straighten out some pots of perennials in a wheelbarrow and then move it back until it was out of the way. He wiped his hands on his pants and turned back to Marsha. "OK, so what's your definition of vision?"

Marsha was perplexed. "I'm not sure where you're going here."

Gardener sighed. "OK. Do you have an idea of how you want your future to be? Have you ever thought about what you want to create with your life—with your sales career? Have you ever thought about why you are in this game?"

"Not really," she answered, staring down at the ground. "Just give me my sales goals and cut me loose—that's been my career!"

Gardener nodded. He was beginning to understand where she was coming from. "That's the norm. So many salespeople go right to goals and forget what is really driving them. Heck, it's easy to get burned out this way. Anyone would."

Marsha looked up. "Yeah, but you're asking all the questions here. Now it's my turn. What's your idea of vision?"

"I'll tell you like I used to tell my colleagues at work. Vision is more than a vague idea of your future, or some pie-in-the-sky unachievable goal. Strong vision has details that are so real you can see it, taste it, and smell it. It's one of the most real things you can have."

Sales Seeds

For a vision to be motivating, you must be able to see it in detail.

EVERYTHING I NEED TO KNOW ABOUT SALES

Marsha looked at Gardener quizzically. "Keep going."

"Once you have clarity about your personal vision, you should write it down and put it someplace where you can see it every day. It's so exciting and so invigorating that just having it around on a yellow legal pad somewhere in your office will inspire you!" Gardener was quite animated now. "Isn't that what a vision should mean?"

Marsha nodded. "Yeah, I see your point. You're saying that by having a vision—a tangible one that I can sink my teeth into—it will inspire me and help me regain my passion."

Gardener grinned. "And what else?"

"Well, propel me to action, hopefully."

"Not hopefully," Gardener replied. "Definitely."

Marsha traced a circle in the dirt with the toe of her sneaker while she listened to Gardener. Passion, she thought, he had in spades. Probably vision, too. But she wasn't sold—not yet. "Hey Gardener, what about my company's vision? They're the people who sign my paychecks, right? Shouldn't they have a vision that I could use?"

"Don't you know what your company's vision is, Marsha?"

"Yeah," she joked. "Churn and burn, baby."

He laughed. "That's good—but not what I meant exactly." He thought for a moment, and then his face brightened. "Let's try this: what's your vision for the garden you're starting? You know, how will everything turn out?"

"That's easy," she said, warming to the task. "I see a gorgeous panorama of color on a calm July morning. There are rows of deep green plants, tomatoes, carrots, and peppers. The soil is dark and rich. There are also the fire-engine-red roses that I planted last year. The aroma is wonderful as I stroll through my gar-

Sales Seeds

Envision how you want your garden to grow, draw it, and put the drawing someplace where you will see it every day.

EVERYTHING I NEED TO KNOW ABOUT SALES

den. It's all beautiful, every square inch of it."

Gardener clapped his hands. "Now we're getting somewhere! I can see your excitement coming through loud and clear as you describe it to me. But let's take it up a notch."

"How so?" Marsha asked.

"Tell me, how do you see yourself using that beautiful produce from your garden? And what do you see yourself doing with those vegetables? How will you use your new roses?"

Marsha cupped her chin in her hands, thinking a moment. "My husband and I love to entertain at small dinner parties, where everyone is involved in the cooking," she said softly. "We're all standing around in the kitchen talking and sipping some really good merlot. And on the table is a beautiful vase full of my red roses, with that wonderful aroma."

"What happens next?"

"My guests love the roses and ask me how I grew them. They ask me how I grew such luscious red tomatoes and such succulent peppers. And you know what I tell them?"

"What's that?" Gardener asked.

"That I had so much fun growing them, I hardly noticed how hard it was."

Gardener let a moment pass for that point to resonate. "So imagine if we could translate that breathtaking vision you have of your real garden to your sales garden. What would we have, then?"

It was like one of those cartoons Marsha used to watch as a child, where a lightbulb popped on over someone's head when he got an idea. "Oh, yeahhh," she said, "my sales territory." She bit her lip and mused for a moment. "Let's try this: friendly, accessible customers who return my calls in ten minutes. Customers who buy 100 percent of their medical supplies from me and me alone."

Gardener shook his head. "I said 'vision,' not 'nirvana.' Having perfect customers would be a little like taking your seeds in April, blindly scattering them to the four winds, and having everything come out perfect with no work or thought from you. How realistic is that?"

"Not very," Marsha admitted.

"OK," Gardener said. "So wouldn't you get bored with such an easy life? Isn't it the hard work and challenge of beating off the competition and really driving home a great customer solution that makes it fun for you?"

"That's it," Marsha thought. "The thrill of the chase."

Gardener went on. "What if you were to build a sales activity plan that supports your vision to accomplish those tough tasks, easily and profitably?"

"I know what you're driving at," she said. "I've gotten so focused on the big-ticket sales in my top five accounts that I've almost stopped going for the building-block sales in my second- and third-tier accounts. After all, you need some of those in your garden, too. Solid, steady plants that consistently produce over time."

Gardener chuckled. "That's what having a vision is all about. I remember a guy in my compa-

Sales Seeds

Positive pictures give you energy and create optimistic feelings that will carry you through the day.

EVERYTHING I NEED TO KNOW ABOUT SALES

ny—another territory—who was cruising along at 110 percent of sales quota with four major accounts. No worries, right? But then the bottom fell out when two of his accounts went through acquisitions and spending got really tight. He dropped from number six to number ninety-seven in the company sales rankings; it took him two years to recover. Why did this happen? Because he became so enamored of his results and numbers at his four key accounts that he completely neglected the rest of his garden. Then, when the big yielders failed to produce, he was in trouble. All because he forgot—or never had—clear personal vision."

Marsha nodded. "Got it."

"Good. So let's try that vision again. This time, really see it, smell it, taste it." After a moment he asked, "What are you doing? What does sales success look like?"

This time Marsha was ready. "Well, let's see—I'm sitting with a good customer, having lunch at one of my favorite restaurants. We're talking really easily; she's asking my opinion of a new product. It's not my area of expertise, but she values my point of view anyway. We finish our meal, and as we linger over coffee she tells me about someone in her network who could use my expertise. She suggests that I call this person and offers to introduce me by making a phone call first. That's the kind of relationship I have with my customers. I'm more than just a salesperson—they see me as a valuable consultant, a problem solver, someone they depend on."

Sales is not just about numbers, it's about people. Take care of the people in all your accounts, and their sales will bloom for you later.

EVERYTHING I NEED TO KNOW ABOUT SALES

Gardener chuckled. "Now you're getting it. Keep working it—how do you feel about that picture?"

"Really good; it has meaning for me," Marsha replied.

They continued walking. At the top of the path a young woman waved at Gardener and Marsha. "Oh, that's Maddie, my daughter," Gardener said, waving back. "She helps out on weekends when she can get away. She's pretty busy with her friends and school, but she loves the place. The day I bought it, she called and said, 'I want to be employee number two in your new gardening empire.' Just like her dad with the jokes."

They walked back up toward the garden store. It was warm for mid-April—about 60 degrees and it wasn't even ten o'clock yet.

"Let me tell you a quick story, Marsha, because I really want you to understand this sales garden concept of mine," Gardener said. "About fifteen years before I retired, I was on a sales call one day. It was a big customer with great name recognition, and I really wanted the sale. After about an hour and a half of rapport-building, presenting, questioning, and empathizing, I left the customer's office with a lukewarm response to my closing questions. I felt discouraged and frustrated. Another wasted call—and half a day to boot! But what I had begun to develop, and what has saved me from dejection after such sales calls, was a new mind-set: that I had just planted a seed, that I was not after a sale as much as I was after another opportunity to plant a seed. I really did not have to brace myself any longer. I knew that if I followed up on that call—really took care of the freshly planted seed—the business would turn my way. Sure enough, I lost the original sale, but two years later this account became the third most productive in my territory."

Love the sales process, each sales step is just another seed that needs to be nurtured and followed up on over time.

EVERYTHING I NEED TO KNOW ABOUT SALES

They reached the top of the hill and Gardener greeted his daughter warmly. He introduced her to Marsha and briefed her on what had to be done before the midmorning rush. As Maddie walked away, he turned back to Marsha and indicated two chairs in the shade outside the door.

"You see, with the gardening mind-set, I repositioned my disappointment in the lack of an immediate closed sale with the knowledge that I had planted a seed," he said after they had sat down. "Having done so, I knew I had to take care of that seed so that it would grow and mature into my vision of a thriving plant in my garden. I discovered that I was beginning to love the process again."

"I'd love to feel as if I loved sales again," Marsha mused aloud.

"Everybody would," Gardener agreed. "I also learned that I did not need to have a 'me against them' mentality anymore—an affliction that I'd wager you're suffering from these days. After all, gardeners don't. While gardeners know that it won't be easy, they welcome the challenges of growing things. Sales professionals need to be ready to accept and face those challenges. Their primary problem is that they don't know how to articulate the overall philosophy of growing great relationships. The good news for you is that we can help you do that."

"Sounds like I'm not alone," said Marsha. "I mean, plenty of salespeople face those challenges."

"That's right," answered Gardener. "And that's why it's a good idea to come down here on Saturdays. Believe it or not, I wasn't kidding last week when I said that I've helped other salespeople with the sales garden approach. The ones who get it are just like you—they understand gardening and they love sales. So it's easier for them to accept what I'm trying to get at—you know, like the planning and vision and passion themes we've been talking about today. Some of them are regular customers. They come down and shoot the breeze just as we're doing, and we talk about weather, weeds, fertilizer, and pests. But we could just as easily be talking about sales as we are about planting tomatoes."

"I hope I get to meet some of these 'sales garden' friends of yours," said Marsha.

Sales Seeds

Many salespeople face the same challenges that you do—find them, share with them, and learn from them.

EVERYTHING I NEED TO KNOW ABOUT SALES

"If you keep coming down here you will," answered Gardener. "In fact, here comes one of them right now."

Sure enough, wheeling into the parking lot toward a space next to several pallets of shrubs and trees was a big truck with "Carson Garden Supplies" on the side. Coasting the truck to a stop, and raising a bit of dust in the process, was the proprietor of Carson Garden Supplies, Jake Carson. A burly bear of a man, Jake got out of the truck and ambled over to Gardener and Marsha. "Fertilizer Man, front and center," he said, a big grin crossing his genial, moon-shaped face. "How ya doin', Gardener? And who's the lady you're keeping time with?"

Gardener laughed as he stood up. "Don't mind Jake, Marsha. He's something of a kidder. Only guy I know who still tells 'knock-knock' jokes."

Marsha laughed at the thought of a big fellow like Jake relaying kindergarten-level gags. She rose and extended her hand. "Hi, Jake—my name's Marsha. I'm a customer but Gardener's been kind enough to help me with some of my, ah, career issues."

Jake took off his John Deere cap and wiped a meaty paw across his sweatshirt before shaking Marsha's hand. "Don't tell me you're another student at Gardener Sales Garden University?" he asked with a laugh.

"Looks that way," she said. "Are you in sales, too?"

"Sure thing!" he replied. "Sold auto parts to Ford and GM dealerships for twenty-five years. Took early retirement and invested in my own company. Now I sell fertilizer to folks like Gardener here. Get my hands dirty and breathe in all that fresh air that Gardener keeps raving about."

"Yep," said Gardener, winking at Marsha. "You might say that Jake is the fertilizer king around these parts. In more ways than one."

All three chuckled at the good-natured ribbing, Jake most of all.

"Awww, I give Gardener a hard time and all, Marsha, but he's a real prince—and a real smart guy, too," said Jake. "I knew him way back when through the chamber of commerce. He helped me through some dark times, when I couldn't make a sale, nor did I care to."

Gardener looked embarrassed. "I didn't do anything, Jake. You had it in you the whole time. I just helped draw some of the passion back out again."

"Bull," said Jake. "Gardener's too modest for his own good. He's never gonna get his own gardening show on TV if he doesn't blow his own horn once in a while."

"Now, Jake," Gardener admonished, "I was only kidding about the TV show. You know that."

"Ahhh, you could do it, no problem," Jake asserted. "Better than 'The Victory Garden,' I'd wager." He turned to Marsha.

"Ya see, Marsha, Gardener came along at the right time for me, when I was in the sales slump of all sales slumps, and I was losing the will and energy to fight my way out. I'd been top producer at my company for years, but I sort of drifted a bit after the ownership changed and the new managers restructured the territory a bit. They took away some of my territory, and my sales suffered as a result.

"Instead of thinking like the top biller at the company—like I'd always been—I began losing confidence and started thinking like the low biller at the company," Jake recalled. "I started eating more and stopped taking care of myself. My wife recommended gardening as a way to get up and move around some after work and on weekends. Before I knew it, I was hooked."

Marsha nodded. "So what happened?"

"A few months later I was at a chamber of commerce breakfast. Who was sitting next to me but Gardener. We made small talk, found out we were both in sales and both into gardening, and began hanging out at the chamber breakfasts every week. Lots of potential customers at the chamber breakfasts—eh, Gardener?"

Gardener nodded, amused at how easily Jake could take over a conversation. "Soon enough, Gardener started telling me about his sales-garden philosophy. I was, ah, skeptical at first, but the more I thought about it, the more sense it made to me."

Jake paused to make sure that he had Gardener's and Marsha's attention. "So I started in on the planning part of it. I planned everything—just like I do when I'm planning my garden—starting with my personal vision. Before, it had revolved around being top biller in the company, but since my territory had shrunk, I didn't think I could do that anymore. With Gardener's help, though, I created a new vision, one that not only renewed my energy but was a much more sustainable one!"

"So, what was it?" Marsha asked.

"I had always defined my success on size of territory and number of customers," Jake replied. "When my territory got cut, suddenly my scorecard was all out of whack."

"What did you do?"

"That's where the sales garden mind-set helped so much—I just redefined my personal vision. With the old scorecard, I was so focused on gaining more customers that I was not really developing the business potential of my best customers. So I had to rethink my approach. Gardener helped me to see myself as kind of a Johnny Appleseed. Now I know that must sound a little corny to you ..."

Marsha shook her head and said, "Not so much—I'd like to hear more."

"Well, as I said, I imagined myself to be like a Johnny Appleseed," Jake continued. "My job was not so much being a salesperson as being someone who planted seeds everywhere he traveled—seeds that could be watched and cared for over time. I wanted to develop a wonderful valley of green trees and beautiful flowers. The more seeds I planted, the happier I felt. I was spreading the word about my products, getting deeper into my customers' business. I wasn't after a sale as much as a new friend and a chance to plant a seed. It really took the burden off my shoulders, and I came across to my customers in a more relaxed, natural way. I think they enjoyed talking with me more, and that's what it's about for me—enjoying the process.

"So, I started targeting my best opportunities, taking time to assess my customers' needs carefully and planning two or three calls per day instead of six so that I could really explore their needs in depth. These activities surely beat my old routine, which had been reduced to a daily accounting of where I stood in the last sales contest, or calculating my commissions over and over based on different product combinations."

Jake stopped for a moment to make sure that Marsha was following him. Then he said, "Before I knew it, I was doing it on a regular basis and my customers were responding to it. I felt like I had really found something different, and I began to get the old magic back."

Marsha was enjoying the conversation with her new friends. Still, she wasn't sold on the sales garden concept just yet. "OK, I'm starting to get this. I see how the vision refocus helped you redefine success ... that's what I need to do. This 'sales garden'—

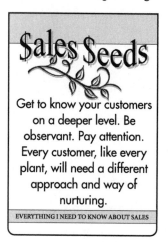

$ales $eeds

Get to know your customers on a deeper level. Be observant. Pay attention. Every customer, like every plant, will need a different approach and way of nurturing.

EVERYTHING I NEED TO KNOW ABOUT SALES

it's a philosophy of sales, a mind-set, that can be applied to any other approach to sales, am I right? And it deals with the bigger picture of how to keep yourself fresh and energized in your career, right?"

"Whoa, you must have been a philosophy major," Jake exclaimed. "You picked that up real fast."

"Faster than you did, Jake—that's for sure," said Gardener.

Another car pulled into the parking lot and stopped near them. Gardener had begun moving some of Jake's inventory into the nursery yard. "Ah, there's Brenda Cobb. Haven't seen her in a while."

Brenda got out of her car, peeling the lid off of her orange juice container and carefully dropping it into a trash can.

"Morning, Brenda. How're you doing?"

"Fine, Gardener. You the same?"

"As always," he replied, angling a dolly full of bird-seed bags against the wall near where Marsha and Jake were standing. "What brings you all the way down here? They don't have a garden shop in your town?" he asked playfully.

"Oh, they do," Brenda answered. "But not one owned by a real live sales sage like Gardener Rawlings. And such a nice shop, too." She turned to face Marsha and Jake. "Hey there, Jake, how's the fertilizer biz?"

"You can smell the success," he answered, to much laughter. He gestured toward Marsha. "This is Marsha Molloy. She's the newest addition to the Saturday Morning Sales Club."

Brenda shook Marsha's hand warmly. "Glad to meet you. In sales?"

Marsha smiled. "Yep. Medical sales."

Jake waved to the group. "I'd love to stay and chat, but I've got some runs to make. I'll leave these bags with Maddie." He hustled over to his truck and unloaded the last few bags of fertilizer. Gardener, Marsha, and Brenda waved to him as he drove off.

Gardener turned toward some bags of birdseed and began moving them onto a pallet. He looked at Brenda. "So why the visit?"

Brenda sighed. "I don't know. I need a little rejuvenation, I guess. The economy stinks and nobody's buying stocks—not from me, anyway. I seem to be losing steam faster than I should be, and losing some business as a result. Got anything for me?"

"Hey, it's Saturday morning, isn't it?" Gardener replied cheerfully. "That's what the Saturday Morning Sales Club is all about." He took a break from the birdseed and sat down on a pile of bags.

Brenda sighed, this time in relief. She'd befriended Bob Rawlings a few years earlier, when she'd sat next to him at a sales seminar in New York. Brash and bold, Brenda had been a high-powered stockbroker for years until the dot-com bust hit in 2000. Most of her customers' money was in high-tech stocks, and they all took a bath. Many customers left Brenda and got out of the market. She'd mentioned that to Gardener, and he was kind enough to help her pick up the pieces and regroup. Now her business was growing again, but not as fast as she'd hoped.

Brenda had already sat down on another stack of seed bags, and Marsha followed suit. Marsha thought the scene comical—three adults sitting on bags of birdseed talking about sales gardens.

"What have you covered today?" asked Brenda.

"We talked a lot about personal vision being the cornerstone of good planning," Marsha answered. "I tend to go straight to sales goals and activity, but Gardener won't let me off the hook on this planning and vision piece!"

"With good reason—planning is a vital component of the sales garden," Brenda said. "I can tell you, without clarity and commitment to my personal vision around the kind of investor base I want, the last two years of bad markets would have put me over the edge! I come here occasionally for a sanity check. Lately I've been having trouble focusing on my plan."

"How so?" asked Marsha.

Brenda thought for a moment. "When things were hot and heavy in the late nineties, I was taking all comers. I see now that I abandoned my value strategy when I started chasing the tech boom—and in the process I let a lot of my long-term–growth customers down. So, with Gardener's help, I redefined what my sales garden should look like: real investors who are serious about steady growth over time—people who are interested in a balanced portfolio. And people who don't go over the top when things are hot or bail out when things are not.

"By reconnecting with my longest-term investors—about 40 percent of my 1999 base—I renewed my personal energy in the business," she said. "But it's been hard. My commissions have been flat over the last twelve months, and it seems that fewer and fewer people want to be in the markets in any way."

Brenda scuffed the ground with her work boot. She looked like a gardener to Marsha. "That's where this Saturday Morning Sales Club comes in handy," said Brenda. "It's a place to kick around what's going on in the world of sales and get the positive support I need. It's like filling up my tank with good fuel for the road ahead."

Sales Seeds

A sales support group lets you hang out with people who are eager to talk and listen, teach, and learn.

EVERYTHING I NEED TO KNOW ABOUT SALES

Marsha nodded. "Yeah, I can see that. I've been down here a couple of weeks now, and it's starting to pay off. For example, right before you got here, Jake Carson was telling me how redefining his vision had changed his career back when he was in auto parts, and how it had set the basis for his new business today. That's pretty exciting!"

"Yeah," said Brenda. "The vision part of planning really helped me, too. But the rest of it also helps—

you know, the seeding and all. The way Gardener explains it, your territory is important and you want it to be the right size, just like your garden. If it's too big, then you risk not having the resources and energy to keep all your customers happy. And if it's too small, you risk not harvesting enough business to keep you going. Is that right, Gardener?"

"Well put," he replied. "But in the planning stage, you have to research what kinds of plants you're going to grow, as well as how big your garden is going to be. In the sales garden, that means studying your customers so that you're not selling them what you have or what you think they should have—you're selling them what they need. You have to find that out first, just like you would learn the likelihood of a good harvest with the seeds you're going to plant."

Gardener looked squarely at Brenda and Marsha. "Good planning means knowing what makes you passionate about selling, as well as who you want to spend your time with, in terms of customers. That's it in a nutshell. Without that clear vision, you're just selling anything you can to anybody who will buy it— and that's a recipe for burnout!"

Maddie walked over with a customer who needed help. Gardener got up to answer her question. Then he turned to Brenda and Marsha. "I'll be right back—I've got some perennials to examine."

After Gardener walked away, Marsha said to Brenda, "I really like Gardener, but does this stuff actually work?"

"It has for me," she replied. "He's taught me a lot about preparation and nurturing my customer relationships—things I wouldn't have normally considered."

"Like?"

"Like with the planning part we're talking about today," said Brenda. "He taught me to make sure that the bigger plants don't overshadow the smaller ones—you know, like the smaller customers. Someday you want them to be big customers, too. But you have to protect them and nurture them. He also taught me not to necessarily harvest everything at once—not to put everything in one basket. Sure, you can plant one kind of vegetable all at the same time and harvest your crop all at once. But there's no reason why you can't plant different varieties and sow the seeds sequentially so that you're harvesting a diversity of vegetables on a regular basis. That taught me not to rely on one or two big customers but to spread out and have different kinds of customers in case one of the big ones leaves—or in a garden—withers up and dies."

"That makes good sense," said Marsha.

"You bet it does," replied Brenda. "Another lesson he taught me was not to be afraid to prune where necessary. It's great to have a lot of customers, but if some are not performing and are taking up too much of your time, you've got to learn to cut them loose so that your other plants—I mean customers—can grow."

Gardener strolled back to where Marsha and Brenda sat talking. His customer had paid for her new plants, and Maddie was helping her carry them out to her car. "See that?" he asked. "She is practicing good nurturing skills with a customer. The customer will remember the extra step Maddie took by carrying her plants out to the car for her. Maddie's persistent—you gotta respect that."

Marsha nodded approvingly. "You're right—but

let's not get ahead of ourselves. I'm still working on the planning thing."

"Of course," said Gardener. "What I most of all want you to remember walking out of here is that a carefully planned garden is much easier to manage. It's going to save you time later on, and it's going to be much more productive than an unplanned garden, that's for sure."

"But you should begin planning your garden well in advance so that when it's time to plant, you're ready to go," Brenda added.

"What else should I be thinking about?" asked Marsha.

"You want to be around positive people, and to stay away from office politics, hostile coworkers, and other salespeople who are negative. They are like weeds that will choke the life out of you—if you let them."

Marsha thought about what Gardener and Brenda had been telling her. "This is good stuff,

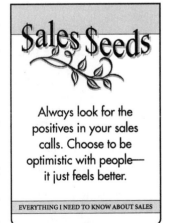

Sales Seeds

Always look for the positives in your sales calls. Choose to be optimistic with people— it just feels better.

EVERYTHING I NEED TO KNOW ABOUT SALES

and I can't wait to try it," she said.

"You'll do well if you plan your garden first," Gardener said, getting up off the stack of birdseed bags and stretching his arms and legs. "Remember, the highest-producing sales professionals are the ones who have clear personal vision and an organized plan they can follow every day. If you have a good plan, you'll be more focused, and you'll also find that your priorities are clearer. You'll start to regain that passion we've been talking about, too, because you'll have a greater sense of purpose and a renewed sense of control over your future."

Marsha got up and dusted herself off. She had a busy day ahead of her, planning her new sales garden, and she wanted to get started right away. "Thank you so much," she said. "Both of you. You've been so generous and helpful."

"Hey, no problem," said Brenda. "Running this stuff by you has been helpful to me, too. It's a good refresher course for my sales garden. Besides, that's what the Saturday Morning Sales Club is all about—helping people to learn what we've learned. After all, we're all in the same boat."

Gardener said, "Oh, and Brenda, maybe the answer to your question of what to do in a tough market is just to go back to your basics, what you do well—increase your seeding from, say, fifty calls to one hundred calls per week. Up that activity level! Something good will happen."

Brenda nodded. "OK, Gardener, will do."

"Great job, ladies," he said. "I'll see you next week. Call me if you need anything in the meantime. And remember, few things make a gardener as unhappy as a garden that lets her down because she didn't cover all the bases in the planning stage. So get planning!"

"Yes, sir!" said Marsha and Brenda in unison, laughing, as they walked to their cars.

 **Gardening Time**

An Afternoon

Thursday afternoon—what a break! One of Marsha's best customers had had an afternoon emergency that was easy to solve, and it left her only ten minutes from home. She would take advantage of the time by getting in an hour in her garden before dark.

As she quickly donned her overalls, she reflected on her week. It had been crammed with meetings all over her territory, so she had already logged about three hours behind the wheel of her car—her "windshield time."

Usually that time was more than filled by incoming and outgoing mobile phone calls, but a funny thing had happened this week. She just couldn't get the conversation about vision and passion out of her head, and she had so many questions. Why was her vision of her garden so crystal clear and detailed, while her vision of her sales success was so undefined (other than in money)? Was there some connection between clarity of vision and excitement about working for that vision? And what about Jake's story of redefining his vision? Was that what she needed to do? "Should I sit back and rethink who my best customers should be instead of relying on the same folks year in and year out?" she asked herself. "Am I short-circuiting the fun of working with some customers for the lure of the big deal? Is that smart?"

As Marsha fed her roses, she made a commitment to herself. In order to be successful, her sales-life vision needed the same level of detail and resolve she had given her garden plan. Now that was something to think about! ❧

Chapter Three

Persistent Seeding

The third Saturday morning of April broke windy and colder. The warm weather that the region had been enjoying recently was a memory. The weather had begun to turn the night before, but Marsha had spent about an hour in her garden anyway, carefully removing some debris that had disturbed a seeded area and making sure that everything was getting enough water—she did this most evenings after getting home, especially in the fragile early growing season.

When Marsha woke up, she could feel the chill in her bones. "I wonder if I caught a cold working in the garden last night," she thought.

But after her initial foray into the sales garden the past week or so, nothing short of typhoid fever would keep Marsha from heading down to Rawlings Garden Supply that morning. With her approach to planning reinvigorated, and with a small sale from an old customer, Marsha already felt that she was beginning to make progress with Gardener's sales garden philosophy. She was aware of being more lighthearted and optimistic than she had been in a long time as she hopped into her truck and headed down to Gardener's store. After a quick stop for some coffee and fresh blueberry muffins, she arrived at Rawlings Garden Supply at about five minutes before nine. Gardener was there with Maddie, sticking tags in the soil of some potted plants.

He nodded at Marsha and walked over to her. "Good morning, Marsha."

"Morning, Gardener—morning, Maddie," she said. Maddie returned the greeting and then picked up a couple of plants and headed out into the nursery yard. Marsha leaned back on the counter and said, "Ready to go, professor?"

"You bet!" Gardener answered. "I thought about your situation last night. I spent some time reading a magazine article about successful salespeople—what they do to sustain their accounts over the long term. It was a good read. You know what I discovered?"

"What's that?" Marsha asked.

"Well, there was a lot about character, integrity,

and ethics. But there was also a lot about persistence—about figuring out what works, and replicating those successful actions over and over—best sales practices, if you will," he recalled. "There was a story in there I especially liked—a case study, I think—on best practices. It was about a salesman who figured that he only had to work so hard once he got an account. Now, I know a million guys like him. They think that all the hard work goes into getting customers. Once you capture the business, they figure, it's all gravy from then on. You know, freebies, long lunches, or whatever else they do to maintain the relationship."

"But that doesn't work," Marsha said. "That never works."

"You're right," Gardener replied. "Shifting into lower gear once you establish a customer base always leads to flat and then declining sales." He grabbed a paper towel from behind the

Sales Seeds

Find out what works, and do it over and over again—repeat it exactly.

EVERYTHING I NEED TO KNOW ABOUT SALES

counter and wiped his hands. "Now, translate that story to our sales garden and what have we got?"

Marsha knew where he was going. "In the sales garden, it's all hard work before and after the seeding—even the harvest. But if you do it right, it's so rewarding. It really can't be any other way."

"I believe so," said Gardener. "But what does the hard-working guy have that those golf course guys don't?"

"Passion?" Marsha asked, hesitantly.

"Exactly. Passion," Gardener said. "If you view the process of taking care of your customers as fun and rewarding, just as we do when we tend our gardens, then you'll take the time to do all that hard work, and you'll do it gladly."

"Because if you don't," Marsha said, "then you'll have an unkempt sales garden that will choke on weeds and bugs and other garden pests. It could even die of neglect. But how do you translate that passion into actual sales strategies?"

"Well, a lot of it rests in persistence," Gardener replied. "If you're persistent in defining your personal best practices—applying those passionately and rigorously with your customers—you'll do better business and build momentum to do even more business."

He took a moment to help a customer find some heavy-duty gardening gloves and some pruning shears. Marsha waited patiently while Gardener joked with the customer and finished the transaction. He waved good-bye and turned back toward her. "So Marsha, what do you think some of those best practices are? What works for you in your business?"

Marsha hadn't thought about best practices much—she was into doing whatever it took to get the sale. "I don't know, being a good listener? Knowing what your customers want?"

"That's a start," Gardener said. "But what I'm talking about is at a different level. I'm talking about figuring out a way to know more about your accounts than any of your competitors do, and using practices that ensure that the account will keep doing business with you, not a competitor."

Marsha nodded. "Yeah, I think I get it. One of the guys I work with religiously conducts

ale eed

Know your customers better than your competition does. Ask for feedback: what's working, what's not, what's next.

EVERYTHING I NEED TO KNOW ABOUT SALES

quarterly business reviews with his top ten accounts—he swears that he always uncovers new needs they have, while getting good feedback on how well he and the company have served the customer over the past three months."

"Good, good," Gardner said. "And I'll bet he only does the talking a small percentage of the time, encouraging the customer to talk more by asking questions and listening. That's what constitutes a good sales review meeting—it frees the customer to talk to you about what's really going on."

When you're with your customer, listen and ask questions 75 percent of the time—that's a best practice.

EVERYTHING I NEED TO KNOW ABOUT SALES

"That's true," said Marsha. "It's so tempting to jump into every interaction with a sales pitch—that's got to be a turn-off at some point. But you see so many salespeople that do it—if they don't have their spiel for the day, they don't know what to do!"

"You know, Marsha, you are so right. That single practice—persistent belief that the customer should do most of the talking and the sales representative most of the listening—is a key determinant of long-term success. Of course, asking the right questions is just as important."

Marsha shook her head. "Yeah ... I guess a lot of sales pitches are like feeding every plant whether it needs it or not—you can kill a few in the process!"

"You got it," said Gardener. "Just that one practice, persistently applied, would go a long way toward achieving successful account sales."

Marsha reflected for a moment. "Hmmm ... like making it a persistent practice to be there the first time a customer tries a product, either in person or by telephone. That surely signals above-and-beyond caring and allows the customer to interact with you at their time of greatest uncertainty."

Gardener gave Marsha the thumbs-up sign. "That's right. Hey, if the persistent use of proven practices works in your garden, why not in your sales life?" He paused a moment and then said, "Come to think of it, I copied down a quote a while back that made the point really well." He rummaged around in a drawer under the counter and brought up a folded piece of paper. "Listen to this: 'Nothing in the world can take the place of persistence. Talent will not; nothing is more common than unsuccessful men with talent. Genius will not; unrewarded genius is almost a proverb. Education will not; the world is full of educated derelicts. Persistence and determination alone are omnipotent.' Pretty good, huh? At the end of the day, wise sales professionals understand and practice that."

Marsha thought, "Oh yeah, Calvin Coolidge. I'd forgotten about that one."

Gardener put the paper away and then waited on another customer. As he finished the transaction, he smiled and asked after the man's family. Marsha thought it was like watching an artist at work, he made relating to customers look so easy.

"You see, persistence is a constant, dynamic process," Gardener said after the customer left. "Right from the start, you're seeding in a persistent and determined way, and then, when you're nurturing, you're listening deeper to what your customers are asking for—even reading between the lines and then checking out your assumptions by asking questions and listening with fresh ears. You've got to think that each customer is different, just like each of your plants, and each needs to be treated individually and with great care."

Marsha knew that Gardener was right. In her opinion, the industry term "Always Be Closing" ("ABC") should really be "Always Be Asking" or "Always Be Listening."

Sales Seeds

Persistence is a constant —you're seeding and following up, and you're persistently connecting to build relationships.

EVERYTHING I NEED TO KNOW ABOUT SALES

Just that week she'd met with a life-insurance agent about upgrading her policy. During the opening minutes of the meeting she was very pleased that the agent was asking all the right questions: What were her life plans? What were her estate needs? She felt good about the guy until he pulled out his sales book about twenty minutes into the meeting, clearly having decided that he had listened enough, and launched right into his rote presentation. Marsha recalled thinking it was as if the timer had run out on his listening and questioning skills and he was going to sell her what she needed. She left the meeting thinking, "This guy doesn't care about me or my situation; he just cares about making his sale, then going to lunch." Her good first impression had changed to a negative one—that the insurance agent had heard it all before and simply did not have the discipline or sincerity to listen to her. Needless to say, the agent did not get her business. She wanted someone who cared about her and her needs. She wanted his full attention even if he'd heard the same story a hundred times. Because for her, it was the first time.

"I see what you mean about persistence being a constant process," she said to Gardener. "I think what makes or breaks a sales rep is being persistent in asking specific questions, listening closely to the answers, and solving problems for the customer until they're happy. It's just like in your garden. You need to be persistent when you're seeding, when you're nurturing, when you're tackling weeds and bugs, and when you harvest. Otherwise, you won't get the results you want, and this piece about knowing your personal best practices and replicating those—that's worth exploring further."

"But a lot of salespeople never realize the importance of persistence," Gardener replied. "Let me tell you something. I had been following a customer for months, making regular phone calls, sending e-mails with information about the industry that might be interesting to her company, and from time to time stopping in for lunch. I thought I had a pretty good relationship going. So I turned my attention to some other new customers who had great potential. When I got back to my original customer—the one I had been following for months—I was told that her company had just purchased a new performance system from a competitor. Hell, I thought, I have a similar system that could have easily been customized to fit their needs! So I asked my customer why she hadn't called me. You know what she said? That they hadn't heard from me for a while and didn't know that I carried this type of product. I had forgotten that customers' memories are often short, and turning away from them—even for a little while—was enough for them to forget about me. Out of sight, out of mind, you know?"

"Oh, brother," Marsha said. "That just goes to show you. I guess we assume a lot about what a customer knows about our products, and how frequently they think about us if we aren't persistently in touch with them." She shook her head. "Sounds like you had a weeding problem there, too, Gardener. After all, somebody swooped in and took your customer's business away when you weren't watching."

Gardener nodded. "Mm-hmm. In the sales garden, competitors are like weeds that are always lurking in the shadows ready to plant their own seeds. Sometimes, when you least expect it, they show up to take advantage of the fertile soil that you have painstakingly prepared. You just turned away for a moment. So after losing that piece of business through neglect, I adopted a practice of always 'touching' every customer twice a month, minimum, by phone, e-mail, letter, sending an article—you know, persistently letting them know I'm out there and very committed to meeting their needs."

Suddenly there was a sound of tires crunching on gravel, and Gardener and Marsha looked up to see Jake wheeling into the

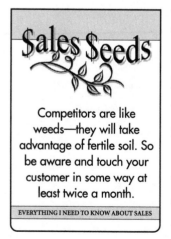

Sales Seeds

Competitors are like weeds—they will take advantage of fertile soil. So be aware and touch your customer in some way at least twice a month.

EVERYTHING I NEED TO KNOW ABOUT SALES

parking lot, gravel flying. "He's going to wreck his car someday, driving like that," Gardener said, shaking his head. He walked out the door, Marsha trailing him.

"Wonder what some of Jake's persistent practices look like—he's in an entirely different business," Marsha mused.

Gardener chuckled. "Well, one thing's for sure— you won't have any problem getting him to talk about them! And I bet they're consistent with the practices we've identified, even though the sales environment that Jake works in is really different."

Marsha smiled as she and Gardener exchanged pleasantries with Jake. They all walked back into the shop, and Jake helped himself to a blueberry muffin. "So what's on the agenda for today?" he asked, to nobody in particular.

"Persistence, old friend—doing what works, over and over because it works," said Gardener. "Something you have in spades, right?"

"You're right about that," Jake replied thoughtfully. "In my business, if you're short on persistence, you're toast. You know, Marsha, a lot of people don't know this, but Walt Disney was fired from his first job. His boss said he didn't have any talent. But Disney persisted, and now everyone remembers him and nobody remembers the boss." He laughed at his own joke, Gardener joining in.

"Seriously, Jake, what practices make up persistence for you?" Marsha asked.

"Honestly, guys, it's as simple as knowing who you want for customers, then getting to know their business better than they do. I know that sounds tough and boring, but that's it for me. In my personal vision, I know what kinds of accounts will yield the 'big deal' results that I want at this stage of my career. And between the Internet, *The Wall Street Journal*, the local papers, and diligently digging for answers when I'm on-site, I'll bet I know more about the business essentials of my customers than most of their employees. I call it 'account profiling.' I know my industry inside and out—not just the people—and I use that business knowledge to go places with my customers that the competition hasn't even thought of. That's how I keep the weeds out!"

Marsha said to Jake, "Wow—that's persistence! I never would have guessed you were that dogged on the business and financial side."

Jake laughed. "Yeah, I guess I don't lead with that, but it's the only way to win over the long term. I watch the wheelers and dealers, and great relationship people ... you know, remembering every birthday, calling the customers' kids by name ... That's all fine, and I do it, too. But you still have to water your plants regularly or they'll wilt on you."

"You know, I had an experience a while back," Marsha said. "I met with a prospect whose company had just branched out into our region. Big potential. So I whomped up a great proposal and made another appointment with her. But she canceled. Tried again. She canceled again. The next time we made an appointment, I just showed up at her office and waited for her. But an hour went by and no sign of her. Just as I was about to leave, she called me on my cell phone in a panic saying that she was down at the hospital with her sick mother, who had cancer and wasn't doing too well. She apologized left and right and told me to wait there—that she'd be back at the office in a half hour. I expressed my condolences and waited just like she requested. Sure enough, she showed up on time. But I made a point of not discussing any business that day. I'd had a sick parent, too, so we talked about that, and how hard it is to see a loved one in so much pain."

The shop was quiet. "It's not that I didn't want the sale," Marsha continued. "Because I did. Very much. But she wasn't in the right frame of mind to talk business, so I didn't bring it up. But the very next day I got a call from her assistant asking for the paperwork to complete the deal. In a weird way, I guess, persistence and sincerity really paid off."

A customer walked into the nursery yard, and Maddie went to see if he needed any help. Jake, Gardener, and Marsha were silent for a moment. Marsha felt comfortable in the silence. Then she spoke again. "Actually, I owe my career in sales to persistence, although I didn't realize it until just now."

"How so?" asked Jake. Gardener perked up, waiting for Marsha's answer.

"I was a senior in college and was graduating in two months. I saw an ad on a job-center board for an entry-level sales rep at a radio station in Boston. I asked an employment counselor there about the job.

He shook his head and said there'd likely be two hundred candidates for such a job.

"I didn't have any experience in radio ad sales, but I knew I'd love the job. Being from the Boston area, I'd listened to the station growing up. All rock and roll all the time. So I sent my résumé in and heard nothing. I re-sent it, and still nothing. Determined to get an interview, I called the radio station directly and spoke with the manager involved directly in the hiring process. She didn't want to meet me at first, but I persisted, telling her how much I loved the station, that my father was in sales—anything I could think of to get my foot in the door. Finally I happened to mention that my uncle taught at Boston University. Turns out the manager had gone there and had taken one of my uncle's classes. Ultimately, I was finally able to pin her down for a time to meet. By this time, though, the radio station had narrowed the original two hundred candidates down to less than ten. Even so, I wound up getting the job."

Gardener smiled. He loved those kinds of stories. Jake was grinning, too. "Why do you suppose they picked you?" he asked.

"I was wondering the same thing," Marsha replied. "I found out later on that the reason the company had chosen me over all the other candidates was that the radio station manager had heard my story—about my repeated attempts to get my foot in the door. Apparently he got a big kick out of it, being a former salesman himself. He told me a few weeks after I was hired that my determination and enthusiasm had made the difference. He said that the main requirements were for someone who was self-motivated, was persistent, and knew how to knock on doors. In short, someone just like me."

"Great story, Marsha," Jake said.

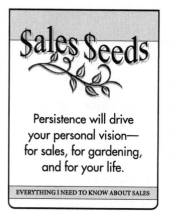

Persistence will drive your personal vision— for sales, for gardening, and for your life.

EVERYTHING I NEED TO KNOW ABOUT SALES

Gardener concurred. "Yep, great story. Let's end it on a high note this week. And let's keep in mind that it's up to each of us to find and replicate the practices that work best for us with our customers."

Gardening Time

Wednesday Midday

Marsha sprinted to her car, having just left a two-hour lunch with Brian, the guy who had chosen her competitor over her company in the latest capital-equipment purchasing process.

Her thoughts were swirling. Just a week ago, she had been ready to disavow having ever known this guy! After all, he had been a customer of hers since the beginning; they had kind of grown up together in the business. He had received two promotions, each one giving him more power to buy more of what she sold. And until last week, the relationship had always gotten her to the finish line.

She started her car and pulled out into the light early-afternoon traffic. It was 45 minutes to her next call, and she had plenty of time to get there, for a change. Instead of putting in her favorite Van Morrison CD, she decided to reflect on the events of the past week—take advantage of a little quiet time.

"To be honest," she told herself, "if I hadn't gone down to Rawlings and had that heart-to-heart with Gardener, would I have done what I did today? Let's look at this closely: Here's a long-term customer who's finally in a position to give me the deal of my

dreams, and what does he do? He gives it to a competitor—and not just any competitor, but the competitor that he knows I like the least! I was livid!"

She veered onto the expressway, her mind a blur.
"My normal MO would have been not to speak to
this customer for a month, at least. Instead, on Mon-
day morning, with the 'vision' of my sales garden in
mind, I started thinking differently, and by 2 p.m.,
to my amazement, I picked up the phone, called
Brian, and invited him to lunch at his favorite spot
... hmmm.

"Brian's initial reaction had been surprise, then
feigned outrage—'You're not planning an ambush,
are you?'—and then acceptance. 'Well, sure, I would
love to!'

"And it couldn't have gone better! Sure, we talked
about the unpleasant stuff—why I didn't get the
business—and to my surprise, I learned something.
Brian had gotten some pressure from above not to
have all of his business with one company—mine!

"And the funny thing was, when I thought of
Brian and his business, which is growing fast, and
his statement that he sees me as integral to the
future success of his business, well, I hate to say it
but the garden metaphor applies. Sure, I have some
growing pains. And my 'harvest' has been temporar-
ily derailed. But as long as I stay persistent and rely

on my strong relationship with Brian, my garden will thrive—and I have a new 'best practice' to boot!"

As Marsha pulled into the parking lot for her next call, she thought. "Maybe there's something to this gardening thing after all!" 🌱

Chapter Four

Nurturing Pays Off

Marsha Molloy woke up on the fourth Saturday morning of April feeling better than she had in weeks.

She opened her bedroom window to let some fresh air inside and felt the reassuring warmth of spring drift into her bedroom. Birds were singing, the sun was shining, and some of the boys down the block had already begun playing baseball—she could hear them shouting and laughing. It made her feel good.

Funny thing about baseball, she thought. Here, all the talk between Gardener and the rest of the gang from the Saturday Morning Sales Club had been about planting and nurturing and growing. And that was fine—in fact, she'd really enjoyed the visits down to Rawlings Garden Supply and relished the one she had coming up this morning.

But something had struck her while watching an old show on ESPN Classic television with her husband the night before. It was a profile of baseball legend Pete Rose. In one segment the reporters were talking to Rose while he took batting practice. One questioner, noting that Rose needed ninety-seven hits to pass Hall of Famer Ty Cobb as the all-time baseball hitting champion, asked Rose how many at-bats it would take to get the ninety-seven hits he needed.

"Ninety-seven," Rose answered, slapping another line drive into the outfield.

"Ninety-seven?" replied the shocked reporter. "Why, that means a 1,000 batting average—ninety-seven hits in ninety-seven at-bats. Nobody could do that."

Rose stopped hitting and wiped the sweat off his forehead. "Look, I'm in the confidence business," he said. "I go up to the plate each time confident I'm going to get a hit. No exceptions." He was persistently confident.

It was a lesson in confidence that made a deep impression on Marsha. Sales was a confidence business, too. Maybe the ultimate confidence business. She'd lost sight of that lately, and in the process she'd lost confidence in herself as well.

She recalled Rose ending the interview by saying that as long as he was prepared and had a plan, there was no reason why he shouldn't get a base hit every time he stepped into the batter's box.

Why shouldn't it be the same for Marsha? Sure, she knew she couldn't close every sale. But she could believe that she could eventually get every customer of hers to sign on the bottom line—but only if she believed in

Sales Seeds

Salespeople are in the confidence business— they need to expect the best from themselves every time.

EVERYTHING I NEED TO KNOW ABOUT SALES

herself. After all, there was no point in meeting a customer if she didn't think it would result in a sale at some point in time. That would be negative thinking, and negative thinkers don't last long in the sales game, sales garden or not. Even just in the last two weeks, Marsha thought, she'd felt more confident and it showed. Now if she could only keep it going.

She padded into the bathroom to wash up, feeling calmer about things. And maybe a bit more determined, too. Splashing some cold water on her face, Marsha mused that it felt as if something inside her had changed already, as a result of her visits with Gardener. Her talks with him, and with Jake Carson and

Brenda Cobb, had changed the way she looked at her career and herself. Maybe it was just having positive people to talk with, but Marsha had begun to see things a bit more clearly—the Rose interview was a good example of that—and she now felt that she just might be ready to tackle the world once again. If nothing else, that was a change for the better.

Outside in the backyard, the plants in Marsha's new garden were growing steadily, and seeing them always brightened her mood. When Marsha had planted some of the seeds she had bought at Rawlings the day after her first talk with Gardener, she followed his instructions closely, careful to look for the sunny and shady areas of her yard as she chose a good patch of land, and careful to space out the seeds properly. It hadn't rained in a few days, so she stopped on her way out to the truck to water her garden before she left.

She unraveled the hose, turned the spigot on, set the nozzle on a gentle spray, and began to water. She'd always liked the early spring season—the return to flower and vegetable growing. She liked how the blooming of her dogwoods and azaleas coincided, without fail, with the return of the robins that flitted about her garden. "Now that it's daylight saving time," she thought, "there's more daylight and more time for me in my garden." As she watered, she noticed that there were aphids on her roses and some of the leaves on her lettuce plants were a little frayed. "Damn!" she thought. "Slugs." She made a mental note to buy slug traps and insecticidal soap from Gardener. She also noticed that some weeds had cropped up among her plants. Sighing, she bent down to pull them.

She finished her watering, taking particular care with some parsley and basil plants that a neighbor had given her. Soon she'd be cooking with them—if the insects and weeds didn't get them first.

Twenty minutes later, after a quick stop for some dark-Peruvian-blend coffee and a bag of fresh egg bagels with some honey-flavored cream cheese, Marsha found herself sitting across from Gardener in his small office behind the counter area, watching him go over his list of things to do for the day. Maddie wasn't in yet, but the store was open. She marveled at how relaxed Gardener was—if someone came in, he'd reasoned to her earlier, they'd find him back here. He didn't seem worried that they'd run off with the cash register. "My customers wouldn't do that," he said.

She sipped her coffee while Gardener finished his list, and then they went back into the store. She picked up a few slug traps, a bottle of insecticidal soap, and another bag of compost, and took them to the counter.

Gardener rang them up for her. "Ah, trouble in garden paradise?" Marsha shrugged. "Yep. Some bugs are eating away at my vegetables. And I noticed some dandelions and some other weeds, too."

"Good. Good." Gardener said, rubbing his hands.

"What? No way that's any good," Marsha said impatiently.

"Sure it is. Don't worry—we'll get rid of your garden pests. But it's a good lesson for your sales garden, too. Think about it."

Marsha sipped some more coffee. "You mean that I'm going to have tough times in my sales garden, too? Some pests and weeds to deal with?"

"Exactly," Gardener said. "In a nutshell, do you always do the right thing when the going gets tough with a customer? Their problems are your problems."

"Let me see," said Marsha. "I guess it stands to reason that if gardens have unexpected challenges—bugs, weeds, disease, storm damage—so does my sales garden?"

Gardener nodded. "That's right. I remember once when we had a customer for whom we did six to nine months of intense project work. Loaded with confidence, I called the primary buyer to ask how we were doing. Her response was, 'I don't really know for sure, yet.' That threw me off, because we were getting great feedback from everyone else at her company. When I asked for clarification, she went on to say, 'I won't really know how good you guys are until something goes wrong. Then we'll find out based on how you respond!' "

"Talk about good lessons," Marsha said.

"Mm-hmm," Gardener replied. "She wasn't going to give me the thumbs-up until she saw me deal with her account when things got tough. She wanted to see how persistent I was in a crunch. That really helped me get my head screwed on straight. Actually, it helped me secure one of my best accounts."

"How so?" Marsha asked.

"I was visiting one of my newer accounts—a surgeon at a big-city hospital. I was in the operating room during three surgeries to evaluate my company's products for adoption by the hospital. The hospital had given most of its business to a competitor because one of the hospital's high-profile doctors had a history with them. The surgeries were scheduled from 2 to 6 p.m. Unfortunately, something went wrong with the last surgery, although it was not related to my products at all. I called my wife to tell her I was going to be a little late." Gardener chose his words carefully. "Anyway, the surgeon finished the procedure around 10 p.m., and after the patient was taken to the recovery room, he stayed at the hospital until he knew the patient was out of the woods. I decided to stay with him. By the time we left, it was about 1 a.m. We went to the parking lot and smoked cigars together and unwound until 2 a.m. He really appreciated my sticking with him all that time, and having the opportunity to debrief and relax when everything was over."

"What did your wife say when you strolled in at 2 a.m. smelling like an old cigar?" Marsha asked.

"Was she ticked off? Yes," Gardener said. "But had I

cemented a customer relationship for life? You betcha! Besides, my wife wasn't complaining when I took her to Hawaii on the first commission check I got from that customer."

Marsha laughed. "So that's important—seeing a distress situation and going several extra miles with the customer until the situation is right."

"Yeah," said Gardener. "And in this case, I won twice. The doctor with whom I'd had the cigars became a customer for life, but when the word got back to other doctors that I had hung in there— including the high-profile doc who was loyal to the competitor—more doctors began to use more of my products, too. It was really nice. I guess you could say that I converted a major 'weed' in the garden into a perennial!"

Marsha scrunched her face. "What does that mean?"

"Well, the whole idea behind 'sales pests' is that they are folks who choose to do business with my competitors. My job is to get those pests working with me. Usually I do that through word-of-mouth about my persistent application of best practices. Once they see the light and convert, they are now productive participants in the sales garden—at least from my point of view."

He stretched his arms overhead. "C'mon, let's go outside—too nice a day to waste indoors."

As they walked among the beautiful blooming plants in the nursery, both Marsha and Gardener began to recount examples of relationships won and lost on the basis of doing or not doing the right thing when the chips were down.

"I remember early in my career being in heavy competition for an account that I really wanted," said Marsha. "I had some business there, but only 10 to 15 percent. I really worked to get the bid for the bulk of the business, and thought that I had earned it based on all the selection criteria. When they awarded the contract to my competitor, I was crushed."

"What did you do?" asked Gardener.

"I got even," she said. "I scratched them off my 'active list'—I didn't even speak to them except to take the occasional order—for months."

"And where did that get you?"

Marsha stopped walking for a moment. "It got me exactly what I deserved—even less business than before. If I had been practicing your sales garden philosophy, I would have viewed the loss of that one six-month contract as just a storm—something that simply required me to go in and repair and restore—and continued my process toward gaining sales in that account.

"Because I didn't do any of that—I just sort of gave up on the whole deal—my competitors are still pretty firmly entrenched in there, and I'm not."

"Yep," said Gardener. "It really is the ultimate test of a great sales professional—how they look at the setbacks, the mistakes, the little perceived injustices, and react quickly to return the climate to one of mutual win-win. Unfortunately, by the time most of us get that, we are at or near the end of our careers!"

"I know," sighed Marsha. "That's a good lesson. The hard part is knowing when that disaster is about to occur, and being prepared to act when it does occur."

Marsha and Gardener strolled onto a walkway

leading to the maze of dirt paths and sidewalks, all framed by plants, that spread out from the store like spokes from the hub of a bicycle tire.

Gardener veered down one of the paths toward the giant greenhouse that held his inventory of heat-loving plants. When they reached the nursery, he opened the door and they walked inside. Almost immediately Marsha's senses were overwhelmed by the fragrance of jasmine and gardenias and dozens of other flowering plants. While it wasn't exactly cold outside, she felt ten degrees warmer just by walking in the door. The sun shone through the clear glass arches that bracketed the building, bathing it in a rich, warm glow. Marsha had always liked the immediacy of walking into a greenhouse. She felt that the warmth and scents inside were signs of nature at work, in harmony, growing things. "Smells great in here," she said.

Gardener nodded. "Yeah, smell the orange blossoms. Lovely."

They walked down the first aisle, which was loaded with fuchsias. "You see, Marsha," he said, "the part about anticipating setbacks and being prepared to act is just like the careful listening that you do to weather reports during our storm season, and thinking through in advance what actions you will take to protect your garden.

"In our customer relationships, we are often so busy listening for the old proverbial buy signal that we tune out the rest of the weather report—a big mistake. There's listening and there's listening. And it pays to look for and listen to any needs information—whether or not it relates to what you're selling. Sure, you can hear a customer tell you he wants thirty boxes of thermometers, if he tells you that. But what if there are other issues—and there always are—that are on his mind and blocking his business success?"

Gardener bent down to pick up a small pot that had fallen off one of the tables. He gently put it back in its place.

"That's where a salesperson who is a good problem-solver comes in," he continued. "Let's say your customer mentions that he wants something to help his medical practice move patients more quickly through the accounting system. There's an opening for you, because while the customer has expressed a direct desire to solve a problem, he's not sure how to

Sales Seeds

Build a reputation as a problem-solver and your customer will value you all the more.

EVERYTHING I NEED TO KNOW ABOUT SALES

do it. So he may present the information in less direct ways."

"I'm not sure what you mean," Marsha said.

"Well, he may complain to you about the delays his practice is having in routing people through the system," Gardener replied. "Or he may relay a suggestion from one of his staffers about cutting paperwork, adding that it was a good idea. Or he may cite a specific patient's situation where the paperwork is notoriously slow, and somewhere along the line of patient, HMO, and doctor's office the right information isn't being relayed in time to meet the patient's—and the practice's—needs."

He picked up a square pot full of budding African daisies. "Let me show you what I mean," he said. "Do you see the plant tag sticking out of the soil?"

Marsha nodded.

"On the back it has some tips on how to care for the plant," Gardener said. "Look at these three small boxes. One says 'full sun;' another 'partial sun;' and the last 'shade.' The box is saying, in the tiny amount of space it has to say it, where to plant the flowers."

He pointed to the term "full sun" on the tag, which had a long black check mark in the box next to it. "That means the plant should get as much sun as possible, at least until the weather turns hot," he said.

"So the tag is telling me that it's a sun-loving plant?" Marsha asked.

"Bingo," said Gardener. "That's exactly what it's telling you, but you have to interpret two or three key words, and you have to have some prior knowledge of the plant, just like you would any customer you're dealing with."

"OK, but growing isn't just about listening—or even reading tags in a potted plant," said Marsha.

"True enough," Gardener replied. "Growing means a lot of other things besides listening. I remember when I first started using the sales garden as the foundation for my sales career. I made sure that I was diligent about planting the right seeds in the right places, and that the seeds had plenty of water and the right care. As the plants grew, I got rid of weeds that threatened to choke them. Most of all, I recall having to

have the patience to allow my sales garden to grow—
it was a long, slow process that had a huge payoff in
the end, if I was a good enough gardener.

"But at the end of the day, gardening requires us to
drop what we're doing and go out and do the right
thing to protect our plants—and so does your sales
garden. All the listening, planning, and anticipating in
the world won't preclude that rough time when what
you do—or don't do—makes all the difference in the
world come harvest time!"

Gardener stopped for a moment and peered
through the large glass windows, up the walk toward
the back of the store. "Good, he showed up."

Marsha looked in the same direction and saw a
man walking down the path toward the greenhouse.
He looked like one of Gardener's typical customers—
he wore broken-in chinos and a bright flannel shirt,
with hiking boots. His neatly cropped black hair was
thinning slightly.

Soon the stranger entered the greenhouse. "Hello,
Gardener," he said. "I knew I'd find you in the greenhouse today. Looking after our jasmine and our
orange trees, are we?"

"Well, it is almost May," Gardener replied. "Everyone wants the best selection of the summer flowers, so we'll be busy today. And I'd better be ready."

The stranger looked over at Marsha. "And hello to you as well."

"Hey," she answered cheerfully. "I'm Marsha. Marsha Molloy. Friend of Gardener's."

"Oh, I know who you are—you're the reason I'm here, from what I understand," he said. "Gardener tells me you're the latest member of our little club. My name's Ted—Ted Santos. I used to work with Gardener a few years back."

Gardener gestured to a couple of benches and they all sat down. "Ted was one of those young fellas who thought he knew everything—just like we all were at one time or another," he said. "He worked in my office when I was just a few years away from retirement. He was a good seller, but he sometimes had a hard time keeping customers."

Ted laughed. "Yeah, I lacked what we call the 'human relations' credentials these days."

Gardener laughed. "Same old Ted," he said. "I asked Ted to join us today because he was able to turn things around for himself and learn how to relate to his customers and listen to them. As part of our firm's mentoring program, I was asked to meet with Ted to see if we couldn't iron out a few wrinkles. As it turned out, Ted was a tough case. He wasn't into gardening and didn't want to hear anything about a 'sales garden' or planting seeds or nurturing flowers."

Ted shrugged good-naturedly. "What can I say? I was a dinosaur—still am in a lot of ways. I figured gardening was for little old ladies in white gloves and safari hats with pictures of birds on them. I liked Gardener—don't get me wrong—but I didn't see how he was going to help me out."

"If you don't mind my asking, what was your problem, specifically?" said Marsha.

"Like Gardener said, I thought I knew everything," Ted answered. "I didn't listen to my customers. I told them what we had in our inventory and tried to sell them what we had, not what they needed. I was good at bringing in new customers, but I couldn't hang on to them because they thought—and rightly so, I might add—that they were just a commission check to me. I didn't get to know them or have patience with them. And I definitely wasn't tuned in to their problems. So when the going got tough, I usually did exactly the wrong thing, and got myself and my company into a hole that we were continually climbing out of."

Ted had been one of those technology whiz kids who came along in the late 1980s when the personal computer was just about to break out commercially. He was one of the first salespeople to have a cell phone in his car and, a few years later, was one of the first to have a portable handheld computer to keep track of his customers. Thus, he was well equipped to handle the mounting demands of managing busy customers from a logistical sense, but not a human sense. "I had all the gizmos and gadgets, and that impressed people for a while," he added. "Heck, it impressed me, too. In fact, I was so impressed with myself that I totally missed out on the nurturing and growing part of the salesperson-customer relationship that Gardener is always so hopped up about."

Gardener interrupted him. "Hopped up about for

good reason," he said, pointing a finger for emphasis. "But Ted bought into this 'total customer management' approach that made the rounds in the 1990s, which emphasized computers and software and cell phones but had nothing to say about one-on-one, face-to-face contact—the kinds of meetings where you get to know your customers and hear their problems."

Marsha instantly felt sympathy for Ted. She, too, had collected all the high-tech tools in her sales career. The cell phone, the BlackBerry, the Dell laptop she took with her to sales seminars and road trips. She was never out of touch with her customers. But from what Gardener was saying, she was never really in touch with them, either, if Ted's experience was a barometer.

"Don't get me wrong," Gardener said. "I think you can grow your sales business by using faxes and e-mails and cell phones." In fact, he'd reflected from time to time on how it was apparent that no salesperson would succeed these days without the toys and tools they used to keep in touch with their customers.

"But they're just one component of your sales business."

Ted nodded. "That's right. And that's how I became a believer in the sales garden. Gardener taught me that expanding my business and keeping more of my customers was a lot like caring for a garden. Sure, you needed the organized systems and the database to keep track of everything, and you needed the cell phone and the e-mail to stay connected.

"But I finally figured out that the difference was continuous, special care of my customers, with a good dose of dedication and, yes, persistence to understand what my customers wanted from me so that they could thrive, just like Gardener and all his pumpkin patches."

Gardener looked on bemusedly. "Ah, Ted, I don't have any pumpkin patches. Never have, actually."

Ted shrugged. "Whatever … you guys know what I mean."

Marsha laughed at the interplay between the two salesmen. She always liked the ribbing and teasing that went on in the business and realized that she had gotten away from the fun and games of being a salesperson, too. It was nice to have some of it back for a change.

Gardener cleared his throat. "But what really helped Ted was that he had a 'failure is not an option' attitude. He sunk his teeth into a problem and wouldn't let go until it was resolved. And once he got persistence down—Ted never had a problem with personal vision—he began to do the right thing in crunches and to pay attention to establishing personal best practices. I think customers noticed that—right, Ted?"

Ted nodded. "I think you have to have a persistent mind-set if you're going to succeed in sales. It's a tough business with a lot of bumps and bruises in it. You can't turn persistence on and off like a light switch, either. It's like in a garden. Real nurturing is paying constant attention to your plants, knowing when they need water or when you need to prune them. And you have to stay persistent when problems like weeds, bugs, and storms arise. That's the real test of a gardener, and it's what makes a great salesperson.

"For example," he said, "one of my customers had

to make a presentation to upper management to gain buy-in on a project. My product would be only a small piece of the overall project, so I wasn't too involved, but when I realized that my customer had no idea how to make an effective PowerPoint presentation to his management, I knew I had to jump in and

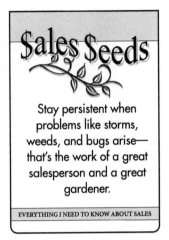

Sales Seeds

Stay persistent when problems like storms, weeds, and bugs arise— that's the work of a great salesperson and a great gardener.

EVERYTHING I NEED TO KNOW ABOUT SALES

help—not just with my piece but with his entire presentation. I spent a day with him developing slides, graphs, Return on Investment charts—the whole nine yards. It was just the right thing to do, and they bought the project. I got my small sale, but what I really got was goodwill from my customer—I'm still getting referrals two years later. High-tech, high touch—remember that one? Doing the right thing was high touch with my customer."

"I know what you mean, Ted," Marsha said. "To properly grow your sales garden, you should be persistent. But part of being persistent is making the effort to know each plant individually: what it needs, what it hates, and what it thrives on. Each plant in your garden has unique needs, and you have to listen and learn to understand what they are. When you find that out, you can determine what kind of special treatment each plant gets and then give it just the right amount of water, the right amount of plant food, and the right amount of care and attention that will allow you to reap a bountiful harvest. Isn't that right, Gardener?"

Always do your homework. Always check out assumptions. Always be asking questions. Always be defining your customers' needs.

EVERYTHING I NEED TO KNOW ABOUT SALES

"Couldn't have said it better myself," he said. "And you're right. Plants, like customers, each have unique characteristics, and they require various kinds of care and nurturing. But when you can provide that special kind of treatment, your sales garden is bound to thrive."

Ted nodded. "I remember one story my dad told me when I'd just graduated from college and gotten my first sales job. It taught me a lot about the importance of listening to my customers and asking the right questions. My dad was an executive recruiter with his own firm. He'd spent a month or so trying to place this woman in a good sales job but hadn't had much success. She was a great salesperson, but the market was tight and they couldn't get any traction.

"One day he got a call from a magazine publishing company looking for a regional director of sales. He was so excited that he got right off the phone and called his client, and she immediately went for an interview.

"Several hours later the phone rang; the saleswoman was on the other end. It seemed that the magazine publisher produced, ah, adult magazines. 'I can't believe you sent me there!' she screamed into the phone.

"Of course, my father was appalled and was very apologetic. In time, the saleswoman forgot about it, but she used another recruiter to land a job. The lesson learned, my father said, was to always know your customers' wants and needs. And never surprise them with something they don't want or need."

Marsha and Gardener both had a long laugh over the story. "That's a good one, Ted," Gardener said. "I'll have to remember it." He got up and stuck his hands in his pockets. "Spring Rush," he announced. "Got to go meet my public."

Marsha got up, too, and thanked Ted for his generosity in coming down to help out. "Oh, don't think anything of it," he replied. "I need this kind of talk with positive people—it keeps me focused. This is my high touch." He added, "If an old dinosaur like me can change his stripes, you'll have no problem."

"You know," Marsha replied, "I'm beginning to feel that way myself."

 ## Gardening Time

Thursday Night

Gardening in the moonlight—how's that for fun? What a week ... three nights on the road and two days that ended at 7 p.m. But the time had flown! Now it was Thursday night. Eight hours of calls tomorrow, but the now-three-week-old plants really

needed some attention—thus the late-evening gar-
den time.

Funny thing was, she hadn't intended to have a
sixty-hour work week—it just happened. Now she
was reflecting on why.

The biggest reason had to be that she was looking
for the little extras she could do for her customers.
Why, today she had sat down with a supply clerk—
something she had stopped doing years ago, since she
usually met with managers who made buying deci-
sions—over coffee to ask some questions about why
he tended to order more from her competitor than
from her.

What a revelation! It turned out that the com-
petitor showed up twice a week, versus her one visit
every two weeks. As Marsha was about to commit to
visiting more often, the supply clerk voiced his desire
to order electronically.

Even though it was late, Marsha seized the
moment to introduce and train this supply clerk in
her company's state-of-the-art electronic ordering
system. He thanked her for taking the time with
him—a two-hour "seeding" that should yield a nice
crop week after week!

"It's funny," Marsha thought, "how things like
this become second nature when you think about

keeping your 'sales garden' nourished and weed-free. I love thinking about it—this metaphor works. And I'm really having fun watching my customers appreciate my new way of doing business!" ॐ

Chapter Five

Harvesting and Renewing

The leaves and stems fell into Marsha's basket softly as she thinned out her seedlings. The weather had turned a bit colder, but it was still only April, and after all, she thought, you couldn't expect 80-degree weather this early in the season, could you? The past week's warm weather had been an aberration, she thought, but a happy one at that.

Satisfied that her vegetables were faring well even with the chill in the air, she picked up her gardening tools and carried them back to her shed. On the way she gathered her thoughts about her meeting with Gardener later that morning. They'd agreed to send Marsha off that day equipped with a complete sales garden blueprint that she could use in the real world. "Theory is wonderful," Gardener had said over the phone earlier that week. "But theory that's not put into practice—well, that's not much good at all."

As she continued to discover, most of her customers, who had liked Marsha all along anyway, were thrilled that she had the old enthusiasm and confidence back in her voice. They'd applauded her efforts and her honesty, and a battery of meetings was set up post haste. She knew she'd be very busy in the upcoming weeks, laying the foundation for her sales garden, but she felt good about it. "I feel like I'm making a fresh start," she'd told her manager. "I'm ready to go, and I have some great ideas about growing my business." Her manager, who had been more than a little concerned about Marsha's performance and state of mind lately, was only too happy to have the old Marsha back.

So with a sense of anticipation Marsha pulled her truck into Rawlings Garden Supply's parking lot. She'd made a special stop and picked up a few boxes of Krispy Kreme doughnuts for Gardener, Maddie, and anyone else who might be there that day. With Gardener, you never knew who might show up, she reasoned, asking the counter clerk for a second box of doughnuts.

Maddie greeted her warmly, smiling in delight over the boxes of doughnuts Marsha held out to her. She opened a box right away. Marsha grabbed one for herself and took a bite. "Say, where is your dad?"

"He'll be along," Maddie said. "He had some stops to make on the way, but he'll be here in a few minutes."

"OK," Marsha replied. "I'll walk around for a while until he gets here."

"Don't be silly," said Maddie. "The place is empty and I've already done my pre-opening routine. Let's chat."

"Sounds good," Marsha said. "Let's sit out front and have coffee." Maddie nodded agreeably. They strolled outside and made themselves comfortable in the two Adirondack chairs perched on the deck.

"Ahh, that's nice," said Maddie. "I was out dancing last night until 2 a.m., and I'm beat. Just don't tell my father."

Marsha laughed. "My lips are sealed," she said. "Reminds me of myself when I was your age." Maddie smiled.

"So, your father is quite a guy," Marsha continued. "Always helping people, loves to garden, and a real charmer, too."

"Yeah," Maddie replied, reaching for the cup of coffee that Marsha offered. "He's made a life out of gardening, and I think this store is the culmination of that." She blew on the coffee gently and sipped some. "Don't get me wrong. He made a good living as a salesman, but I think his heart has always been in the land, growing vegetables, planting shrubs, things like that. I think he's at his happiest when he's out in his garden. Or when he's here, helping people to plant their own gardens."

"Why do you think your father is so happy?" Marsha asked. "I mean, he's always laughing, always having fun. What's his secret?"

Maddie couldn't help but smile. "Yeah, everybody says that about my dad. Actually, I asked him about it once. He told me some Zen thing about finding balance in your life. If you have balance, you lead a more complete life. I guess that means a happier life, in his case."

Marsha thought about that for a moment. She knew the importance of balance, but in the hyper-competitive sales game it was tough to find time to do anything else but find ways to close more deals. She made a mental note to bring up balance when she met Gardener later in the morning.

"Did he ever teach you anything about gardening?" Marsha asked.

"Oh sure," Maddie said. "I tried, but I don't think I have the green thumb that you guys all seem to have. But I do like being around the store and helping out. I've learned a lot just by doing that."

"But you remember everything he taught you?"

"Pretty much. Why do you ask?"

"I don't know," Marsha said. "I guess it always helps to get a different point of view."

"Well, my favorite part of gardening is harvesting, if that helps. My dad says it's a lot of work but it's so worth it."

"What didd he teach you about harvesting?" Marsha asked.

"Lots of things," Maddie said. "He taught me not to harvest vegetables too early. Or to harvest in a way that might damage the garden. He's really into details, too. Like, he says that it's OK if you want to plant a bigger garden than you did last year. But if you do, he says, different terrain may require different plants. He also says to make sure that the garden hose will reach

the new plot so the farthest plants won't wither and die. Y'know, little things like that."

You keep your customer's trust by having a balanced harvest—not too early, not too late.

EVERYTHING I NEED TO KNOW ABOUT SALES

"I agree with him—the devil is in the details," Marsha answered. "And I think you should always take a long-term view of your garden—and your life, for that matter."

"Wow, getting deep here, aren't we?" said Maddie teasingly.

"Hey, I'm serious," Marsha said. "Do you know why your dad has all these people coming down to talk with him for hours on end?"

"I think so," said Maddie. "Something about sales gardens, right? For people in business, salespeople, and stuff like that."

"Yeah, and I'm one of them," Marsha answered. "Your dad's been helping me get my head on straight and re-energize my career. And he uses the sales garden metaphor to do it. Apparently I'm one of many."

Maddie gazed down the road to where it curved by the entrance to the state park. "That's cool. I guess my dad is some kind of sales shrink or gardening guru or something. As long as he's helping."

"Oh, he's helping all right," said Marsha, somewhat more emphatically than she had intended. "Like this thing about the sales garden. It makes a lot of sense. Basically, if I can manage my garden, and thus manage my accounts capably, I'll be a solid producer for years to come. It's pretty simple when you think about it."

"I think I know what you mean," said Maddie. "Like, my dad's on me all the time about treating our customers right. If I push the same plants—the ones I know best—he'll come over later and tell me that the best gardens are the ones with the greatest mix of plants. Vegetables, fruits, whatever. He wants me not to promote the same plants, but to mix things up a little. Or he'll

When harvesting, don't be too aggressive. Satisfy your customer's needs, not your own.

EVERYTHING I NEED TO KNOW ABOUT SALES

remind me not to be too aggressive with a customer and try to load them up with a bunch of plants they may not need."

Marsha nodded. "In sales we call that 'overkill.'"

"Yeah," laughed Maddie. "Dad says that if I sell them things they don't want or need, they won't come back. Good for the short term, he'll say, but bad for the long term."

"He's right," Marsha said. "In my line of business it's a good idea to visit the garden often, so to speak, rather than wait until the end of summer. That's neglectful. In sales, regular visits enable me to get to know my customers on a more personal level. And when you do that, you're there to get rid of the bugs or pull the weeds when they arise. Those are the kinds of things that can choke a garden—or a sales career, for that matter."

Maddie looked over at Marsha and smiled. "I don't know that a sales career is for me. But if it is, I'll sure know where to go to get some good advice."

Marsha chuckled. "Yeah, and you can start with your father."

Two cars pulled into the lot. "Customers," sighed

Maddie. "Shouldn't have hit the dance floor so hard last night." She got up and went into the store to get ready for them.

Marsha sat for a moment, reflecting on her conversation with Maddie. Not exactly a chip off the old block, but in a good way. Maddie was different from her father, Marsha surmised—more pragmatic. Probably the type to go off to a good business school like Michigan State or Penn and learn how to manage people.

Deep in thought, she was startled by the sound of a familiar voice.

"Hey, lady, no sloughing off at Rawlings Garden Supply." It was Gardener, standing over Marsha with a big grin on his face.

"Yep," said Marsha. "You can't rest on your shovel. Any goldbricking and my garden will turn into a weed festival." How true, she thought, as soon as the words left her lips. Gardens and customers experience neglect in the same way. They see it as indifference and as a result stop growing.

Gardener looked on bemusedly. "Boy, I wish you could hear yourself. Nothing like the sourpuss who came into my store a month ago. Belly full of fire and ready to go, aren't we?"

"I'm getting there, thanks to you," Marsha replied. "Everything I needed to know about sales I learned from my garden, right?"

"I like that," said Gardener. "C'mon inside. Let's get a hot cup of coffee."

Gardener and Marsha went inside. She waited patiently while Gardener went over the day's to-do list with Maddie. Then he helped a customer pick out a shovel and a wheelbarrow and rang up the purchase. "OK," he said when the customer left, "I've got some free time. Let's hang out in the shop today—a little too cold out for me this morning."

"Fine," Marsha said.

"So what's on our mind this week?"

"Um, I had a nice chat with your daughter this morning."

"Oh boy," Gardener chuckled. "She didn't give away any state secrets, did she?"

Marsha shook her head. "No, nothing like that. But she did mention that she thought you were leading a happy life. She said you had balance in your life, and that was the key."

"Do you know what she meant?" he asked.

"I think so. If you can find the right balance between work and family, between material wealth and spiritual wealth, life's much easier to handle. Is that pretty much it?"

"Well, it all goes back to the sales garden, doesn't it?" Gardener said thoughtfully. "It's like when you grow your sales garden and you're wondering when is the right time to harvest. You've got to realize that there's a balance in your sales garden, too. Just like in the sales business. We're always in a tug-of-war of sorts with our customers, our bosses, our companies. Now why do you suppose that is?"

Marsha sipped some coffee and considered Gardener's question. "You know, I was thinking about that this week. I was in a meeting with our director of sales, and he was going over the quarterly sales quotas. He was really pushing the quota, and I found myself defending my turf a bit."

"How so?" asked Gardener.

"I told him that I understood the company's obligation to its shareholders, and how meeting our quotas was a big part of that obligation. That said, I explained to him—you would have been proud of me, Gardener—that some of my customers weren't ripe for picking yet. That if I tried to harvest them now to meet some artificial deadline, I might make a sale, but I would lose their trust and confidence over the long haul."

Sales Seeds

Don't be afraid to advocate to those around you for what you believe is the right thing to do.

EVERYTHING I NEED TO KNOW ABOUT SALES

"You used a gardening analogy in front of the director of sales?" laughed Gardener. "Oh, that's rich, that's a good one."

"What's so funny?" Marsha asked. "It was perfectly appropriate. The thing is, he agreed with me. He said that balancing the needs of the company with the needs of the customer was a critical issue for salespeople."

"And what did you say?"

Marsha smiled at the thought of it. "I said that he was right. That you wouldn't pick an unripe tomato a week in advance to meet some technical goal of having more tomatoes every week."

Gardener clapped his hands and guffawed. "Bingo! That's the ticket. My student is now a teacher! Best way to learn, I always say!"

"That's not all," Marsha said. "I also told him that, on the other hand, you wouldn't leave two ripe tomatoes on the vine because you already had five of them. When they're ready to be picked, I said, then you pick them. Not a moment too soon and not a moment too late."

"Houston, we have balance," joked Gardener. "The sales world these days is full of tactics to get customers to buy more than they need to meet end-of-year or end-of-quarter sales targets. Let me tell you a story."

Marsha looked over at Maddie, who was rolling her eyes in mock exasperation. Marsha laughed.

"Oh hush, both of you," Gardener said. "As I was saying, I was faced with a real dilemma one time. I was only $30,000 short of making my bonus in the third quarter. One of my top accounts needed sixty units of my product in the fourth quarter and wanted to buy them twenty at a time, on the first of every month. If memory serves, I think it came out to $10,000 per month, billed on the 30th of the preceding month. Typically, they had bought all units on the last day of the preceding quarter, so I had been counting on the $30,000 as the ticket to get the extra 5 percent.

"To make matters worse, we were getting major heat from corporate to beat our nationwide sales plan, and our third of the country was vying for top-area-of-the-quarter honors, which meant some nice incentives for all of us.

"Since I only had three days left in the quarter, and the customer's proposed solution—to bill per month instead of in advance for the quarter—got me $10,000 of the $30,000 I needed, I was sorely tempted to push for the whole $30,000 right then and there," Gardener recalled. "After all, that's how it was done in the industry back then, and probably how it's still typically done.

"Then I thought about whether I could get the $20,000 somewhere else. I checked my sales garden and figured that with some extra work, the answer was 'probably.' I realized that I could build some goodwill with my customer by handling the billing issue the way they wanted."

"So what did you do?" asked Marsha.

"Well, as we discussed last week, in a crunch, do the

right thing by the customer. As it turns out, the customer had changed their buying procedures so that purchases over $15K had to be screened by their purchasing group—a process that would invariably lead to some kind of open competitive bid process every quarter.

"By agreeing to the shift, I allowed my customer to avoid this internal screen, which was good for both of us. Better yet, he was willing to guarantee in writing another twelve months' purchase for that particular product at $10,000 per month. And sure enough, with a little diligence I found that $20K elsewhere in my sales garden, and got the 5 percent bonus."

He looked over at Marsha. "Now, how about that for a win?"

"That's easy," Marsha said. "It means that the timing of the harvest is everything. Do everything you can to ensure a speedy and robust one, but the produce must be picked on its schedule, not yours."

"Excellent," Gardener said, rubbing his hands in satisfaction. "Now, are you ready to harvest your sales garden?"

Marsha nodded. "I think I'm ready for the harvest—at least the harvest lesson, anyway."

"Ah, I love the harvest," said Gardener. "It's like closing a million-dollar sale. All that preparation, all that hard work, and then bam! The payoff!"

"Love the payoff, that's for sure," said Marsha. "But how does harvesting fit into the sales garden?"

"Good question," said Gardener. He pulled up a wooden stool and offered it to Marsha. Then he sat on the counter. "We all know that the last step in the sales dance is the close," he said. "Unlike the planting and nurturing process, which takes a long time, the close should be done quickly. In a garden, you've tended to your vegetables as best you could. When it's harvest time, you're essentially asking them to reward you for your efforts with a bountiful crop. If you've done your homework, they do just that."

He took an apple from a basket on the counter and took a big bite. "Keeps the doctor away," he said, chewing slowly and savoring the taste. "Anyway, it's the same deal in the sales game. You've identified your prospect, sowed your seeds, watered and fertilized and weeded, and paid attention to what your customer was telling you. Now it's time to ask for the business and sign on the dotted line.

"But that doesn't mean you can ask anytime you want," he continued. "No, no. It's like that story I just told you. You can't harvest too early and you can't harvest too late. You have to harvest at just the right time. If you try to harvest your sale too early, the customer may not be ready. Too late and some nasty crow might have swooped down and stolen it from under your nose. But if you time it just right, like I said, lickety-split, they sign on the dotted line. That's the issue when it comes to balance—knowing when the time is just right."

He waited while Marsha let that sink in. After a moment, she looked up. "But how do you know your sales garden is ready for harvest?" she asked.

"That's the great thing about gardens," he replied. "They're nonverbal, true. But they can still speak to you and let you know what they need and when it's ready for you to reap what you sowed. It's just a matter of knowing the nuances of your garden, or in your case, your customer. Let me explain.

"Good salespeople are experts at the communications side of the game. They put in the time to get to really know a customer—and I mean listening 75 percent of the time for months on end, which many are incapable of doing. But by the time they're done, they can recognize the inflection of a voice over the phone or the look in a customer's eye that says 'Let's do business.' They know it instinctively because they've done their homework. So they know when it's time to harvest because the customer is giving clear 'buy' signals."

"Unless the customer calls up and says he wants thirty boxes of thermometers by next Wednesday," Marsha laughed.

"Yeah," Gardener responded. "We'd all love our customers to be just like that. Unfortunately, they're not. You've got to know their moods and nuances. You've got to read them like a book. Any farmer worth his salt will tell you it's the same thing with his crops. He's spent so much time with them that he just knows when it's time

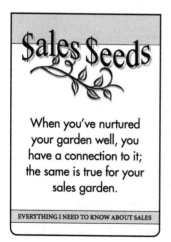

Sales Seeds

When you've nurtured your garden well, you have a connection to it; the same is true for your sales garden.

EVERYTHING I NEED TO KNOW ABOUT SALES

to harvest. It's a connection only a few really understand.

"When it comes to harvesting," Gardener went on, "just like in your garden, some customers may be ready before others, all things being equal. I said that you don't want to harvest early, and that's a fact. But the vegetables you harvest first? Plants like peas, snap beans, beets, and carrots are best taken sooner rather than later. They're the ones that pass their prime quickly. Same with some customers. The ones who are more anxious to do business with you—they're the ones who want those thirty boxes of thermometers you're talking about. But other vegetables, like corn and winter squash, have to wait until they're completely ripe. Those are the customers that you've put more time into and that may have taken more time to ripen. But often, they turn out to be your biggest accounts because of all the extra care you've shown them."

Gardener took a swig of coffee. "The thing with big accounts is that they're like big oak trees. They take time to develop and grow, and they involve a great deal of careful planning. They're steady growers, and they have deep roots and will be around for a long time. So they're worth developing. After all, some seeds take longer than others to grow."

"So," Marsha said, "the trick is to harvest each crop at its prime."

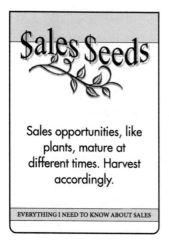

Sales opportunities, like plants, mature at different times. Harvest accordingly.

EVERYTHING I NEED TO KNOW ABOUT SALES

"Exactly," Gardener replied. "That could mean harvesting your lettuce and tomatoes on a daily basis and harvesting your eggplant and potatoes once a week or so. In the sales garden, you can harvest your customers who are ready and accessible more often than you can the ones who don't wish to be contacted on a daily basis or who might be a tough sell. You've got to remember that customers, like plants, mature at different rates. You've got to plan for that and harvest each opportunity accordingly."

"I'm trying to visualize what you're saying," Marsha said.

"Good! Good! Visualization is excellent," Gardener

exclaimed. "Weak and scattered thoughts are worthless and won't do you any good. But strong and focused thoughts that include visualization? That's great stuff. Changing your thinking is a huge part of the sales garden mind-set."

He paused momentarily, lost in thought. "Oh, now I remember! There's a great story about visualization involving the actor Arnold Schwarzenegger, only he wasn't an actor then, he was a bodybuilder. In fact, if I recall correctly, he was a world champion bodybuilder and he won the Mr. Universe title a few times. He said once that he'd actually won those tournaments before they started. He'd walk around the stage and the dressing rooms like he owned the place. He visualized in his mind that he was already the champion. His confidence paid off. He could feel and taste the success beforehand, and the audience fed off it and cheered him the loudest. Geez, I love that story."

"But how do you visualize your sales garden paying off?" Marsha wanted to know.

"Take some time in the morning and visualize your plants growing strong and tall, with sturdy roots in good, rich soil," said Gardener. "Then visualize the harvest. How all the hard work has paid off with such beautiful vegetables. I used to do it all the time when I was in sales, and I still do it with my garden."

"Yeah, I've been working on the vision thing," said Marsha. "I'm trying to visualize the harvest—all the fresh produce I'm going to have and how happy I'll be. Maybe taking some vegetables to my neighbors or grilling them on a barbeque. You know, my company is setting a new bonus plan, and I'm beginning to see myself on the white sands of Hawaii."

"Good, good," said Gardener. "But we're forgetting something else—something very important when harvesting your sales garden. Care to guess?"

Harvest with the future in mind—after your first sale, always prepare for the next one.

EVERYTHING I NEED TO KNOW ABOUT SALES

"The only thing I can think of is the renewal part," said Marsha. "You know, making sure that when you harvest, you're also laying the groundwork for the next planting season."

"That's right," said Gardener. "Right as rain. It's the same thing with your customers. There's birth and rebirth. When you make your first sale, you've got to be thinking about the one after that. That means listening and being persistent in understanding what your customer needs. Remember— always harvest with the future in mind."

Maddie came over with a question for Gardener, and Marsha realized that it was time to go. She waited until Maddie had walked away, and then she told Gardener that she was leaving. She knew it would be busy at the store and didn't want to monopolize any more of his time. "OK," he said. "I guess it's for the best. But remember one thing before you go. A carefully planned garden is the foundation for a great harvest—and for future harvests as well. If you plan your sales garden right, you'll have all the repeat business you'll ever want."

Marsha smiled. "Thanks, Gardener. Thanks a million. Really."

"Oh, don't thank me," he said. "You'll do fine. Plant some quality seeds and nurture them, and you'll see a big change in your business. But work hard. Remember, there are only two ways to get to the top of an oak tree. One way is to sit on an acorn and the other is to climb it."

"I'm a climber," Marsha said confidently.

"Sure. Just do me one favor," Gardener said.

"Sure, anything you want."

"Whatever you've learned here these past few weeks, try to pass it on to someone else who may have the same doubts as you did," he said. "In other words, pay it forward."

"I'll do that, Gardener. In fact, I've started meeting with a couple of other sales folks for early coffee once a week. We call it the Wednesday Morning Sales Club, and it's sort of a midweek pick-me-up."

They said their good-byes, and then she gave him a hug and walked out of the store. She had a lot to do and couldn't wait to get started. She was excited and ready to go! But she knew she'd miss her regular visits with Gardener. Oh, he'd invited her back whenever she felt the need to talk, and she knew she'd take advantage of that often. But deep down inside, Marsha knew that he'd already given her the formula.

Now it was up to her to use it.

Gardening Time

Wednesday Afternoon

After buying her favorite gardening magazine at the airport newsstand, a reward for a satisfying day, Marsha was ready to board her short flight back home. She had in her briefcase a purchase order that exceeded her annual goal for this customer by 20 percent. It was a great feeling—and she couldn't wait to share the news with her manager, and with the folks in her sales clubs.

Marsha also felt exuberant about how her sales harvest had gone this year. Usually, at these kinds of annual purchase-commitment meetings she had all guns blazing to get her customers to order to the max.

This time was different. She had focused on harvesting only what was ready to be harvested—asking questions about real product-utilization needs and generally helping her customer spend their tightly budgeted dollars as wisely as possible.

The best moment came when they seemed to be uncertain about a fairly expensive equipment purchase because of disagreement among the doctors and staff on what model was best for their particular needs. Instead of pushing hard for the sale now—something she would have done in the past—she realized that they just weren't ready to buy today.

So she reached an agreement with the customer that she would go in with her technical expert and demo two or three models for all the doctors and staff, to help them reach the right buying decision instead of a fragmented one. Renewing the soil—adding more value and getting ready for new growth.

Score another win for Gardener! ❧

New Beginnings

Four years later

Marsha Molloy felt as if she were having an out-of-body experience.

She had prepared herself. But when she heard the emcee call her name, all the preparation in the world wouldn't have mattered—she nearly fell out of her chair, anyway. After all, it didn't get any bigger than Salesperson of the Year at the National Sales Meeting Awards ceremony.

Shocked and somewhat humbled, she rose from her seat, accepting a hug from her husband on her way to the stage. She knew the award belonged not simply to her but to her husband, her manager, and, perhaps most of all, to Gardener Rawlings. Marsha also knew that she'd been drifting along until she set foot in Gardener's shop. Without that chance meeting, and the subsequent patience, kindness, and generosity of spirit that Gardener showed her in the following weeks, months, and years, Marsha knew deep down that she'd be lucky to still have a job today, let alone receive this award tonight.

She'd realized something over the past few years: It wasn't enough to want to be happy again, to have fun again, to regain her passion for sales. No, she needed much more than that. She needed that support system she'd had in the Saturday Morning Sales Club. Just as doctors needed to talk to other doctors, writers to other writers, and even—maybe especially—gardeners to other gardeners, salespeople needed to be among their own, sharing experiences, swapping war stories, and bucking each other up when they were down, just as Marsha was before she met Gardener and the rest of the gang.

She recalled from time to time what Gardener had said to her about trying to go it alone. It was the first day she had met him, and they were discussing her fatigue and stress over her career dilemma. She had told him how isolated and lonely she felt. Revealing those feelings to Gardener made her realize that she couldn't do this alone. "It's no fun dealing with sales problems on my own," she thought. She felt noticeably better—almost immediately—after she began meeting with Gardener and the other members. She confided as much in Jake Carson, who lent a sympathetic ear. "Hey, sometimes you need others to help you get unstuck," he said. "Or sometimes you need to talk with somebody who's been through the wars, been through the same things you have. I mean, what do you think the Saturday Morning Sales Club is but a support group for salespeople?"

The comment really hit home with Marsha. She mentioned it to Gardener, who shrugged and then said, "Well, Marsha, why do you think we meet on a regular basis? Why do you think we meet on Saturdays? Why do you think we try to give everyone the opportunity to air their concerns?"

Marsha didn't have any answers at the time. But a few weeks later, she discussed the structure of the meetings with Brenda Cobb. What Brenda said set the stage for Marsha's own growth within the structure of the Saturday Morning Sales Club: "For us to get the most out of these meetings, they've got to have some organization, some structure. Sometimes we might get long-winded and monopolize the time. But someone else will bring us back down to earth and remind us that everyone deserves some time to talk and some time to listen. When you think about it, participating in the meetings is a lot like managing your customer relationships. You do some talking and you do some listening. You have to be conscious of why these meetings work—it's because we all have a role and we're all looking out for each other." That, Marsha decided, was how she was going to approach the Wednesday morning meetings, and from that point forward, that's exactly what she did.

As a result, tonight she couldn't be anything but happy. The award was the culmination of years of hard work, of redirection and focusing like a laser beam on her sales garden philosophy. Admittedly it hadn't been easy gaining traction at first. She'd experienced some fits and starts, especially in organizing a sales plan that allowed her to instill the tenets of the sales garden: the planning, making sure she chose a number of different types of seeds; the planting; the nurturing, weeding, and pruning; and the harvesting and renewing the soil for the next year's garden. But once she got the ball rolling, everything fell into place.

Tonight, she thought, was a night she'd never dreamed would come. She walked up to the dais, feet barely touching the ground. She clutched the gold-framed plaque the presenter had given her and looked out at the people in the audience, many of them her friends, on their feet and clapping wildly for Marsha. She noticed that her boss was clapping and cheering the loudest.

"Thank you," she said, speaking softly at first. "Thank you all so much. Really, thank you so much." The applause abated and the audience sat down. "A few years ago," she began, "I never would have expected to be standing here tonight, accepting this award, in front of you all—people I've always respected and admired. It's a bit of a miracle, frankly.

"I remember a story about the great golfer Ben Hogan. When asked the secret of golf, he answered, without looking up at his interviewer, 'It's in the dirt.' He went right back to practicing hitting golf balls, digging up small chunks of earth with every swing." She paused for a moment to let her words sink in.

"It's in the dirt," she continued. "I love those words. I've taken them to heart in recent years, thanks to a great friend of mine who taught me that the secret of successful sales was, as Ben Hogan said, 'in the dirt.'

"I'd been a successful medical sales representative

for years," Marsha said. "In fact, some of you out there—and you know who you are—gave me the nickname 'Marsha Money,' and for years I tried to live up to that name. But I hit some hard times, and for a while there, I wasn't even sure I wanted to continue in sales. I felt burned out, like it had all been done before and there weren't any more mountains to climb and oceans to cross.

"Worse, I'd lost my passion for the sales business and forgotten the reasons why I'd gotten into the business in the first place: the face-to-face interaction, the thrill of closing a deal, the satisfaction of building long-term relationships.

"Then one Saturday morning I was driving to my garden supply store to get some seeds and some tools for the planting season. My old garden store had gone and a new one had taken its place. The store had a new owner, a retired salesman named Bob Rawlings, who had a nickname of his own—'Gardener.' Gardener was a nut about gardening and crazy about the sales game—he'd been a salesman for thirty-five years before retiring and buying the store. In doing so, he found a way to merge both passions into what he called the 'sales garden'—an approach to growing your business that mirrored the way a gardener would plant, nurture, and harvest her garden.

"Well, without going into the details, that's exactly what happened to me. Gardener, along with the rest of the folks who made up what we called the 'Saturday Morning Sales Club,' helped me get my mojo back. So Gardener, wherever you are, thank you so much, from the bottom of my heart. We did it—we put the fun back into sales, and it couldn't have happened without you."

On her way back to her seat, Marsha recalled that chilly morning in April, four years earlier, when Gardener had reminded her to, as he said, "pay it forward." Determined to make good on her word to help others as Gardener had helped her, Marsha made up her mind on the spot that that was what she would do.

One year later

Marsha was swimming in success and once again enjoying all the perks of being a top producer at her firm and in her industry. It was late February, and, as was her habit, she climbed into her truck one Saturday morning to head down to Rawlings Garden Supply. Planting season was coming soon, she thought. Time to think about putting in her new garden.

Cruising down the blacktop on a crisp, sunny, late-winter morning, Marsha felt on top of the world. She hadn't seen Gardener since Christmas, when she'd attended the store's holiday party. She loved this time of year and looked forward to talking with Gardener about plants and soil and compost. This would be the sixth planting season since she had met Gardener, and she'd learned a bit more about gardening—and herself—each year.

Rounding the curve near the state park, she saw the familiar sign for Gardener's store. As she rolled up the gravel driveway and pulled into a spot by the front steps, she noticed something odd. A sign reading "For Sale" was on the front door in large red letters. Confused and a little apprehensive, she walked up the steps and tried the door. "Locked," she said to herself. "That's odd—Gardener's always here by this time of day, especially on a Saturday, when all the gardening buffs are out and about." Growing more curious by the second, she cupped her hands around her eyes and peered inside. Nothing stirred. Then, just as she was about to give up and head back to her truck, she saw movement in the far corner of the store. Her eyes adjusting to the relative darkness inside, she saw someone sweeping the floor near Gardener's old "Seed Farm" section, where all the racks of seed packets and bags of birdseed were located. "It's Maddie," Marsha thought. "What's going on here?"

She rapped on the glass door, tentatively at first, then a bit louder when she didn't get a response. Finally Maddie looked up, gave Marsha a wan smile, and walked over to the door and opened it to let her inside.

"Hi Marsha," she said. "Nice to see you."

"You too. As always." Marsha glanced around. They were alone. "Maddie, what's going on? I saw the 'For Sale' sign, and I was really surprised. Why is Gardener selling?"

"Well, my dad's been getting tired lately," Maddie said, "and he'd like to do some long-promised travel with mom, so they decided to spend the next couple of years traveling, and they're excited about that."

"That's wonderful," said Marsha, whose feelings were very mixed, "but what about the store?"

"I'm sorry, Marsha," Maddie said. She hugged Marsha warmly. "I don't want to sell, and neither does Dad, but he feels that if he can't put 100 percent into it, he'd rather pass the torch to someone who can. Just the way it goes, I guess."

Marsha took a moment to let the news sink in. She'd come to think of Gardener and Rawlings Garden Supply as a single entity. Without Gardener, could there be a Rawlings Garden Supply? And then she had an idea.

"Has anyone made an offer yet?"

"No—not yet," Maddie said. "I put the sign up this morning, just before you got here."

Marsha stood up, feeling better about her idea every second. "Maddie, I don't want to be presumptuous, but I'd like to buy the store. I owe Gardener, and strange as it sounds, something drew me down here this morning. I feel bad about Gardener selling the store, but maybe if I buy it, we can keep it going." The more Marsha heard herself talking, the more confident she felt that she was doing the right thing.

Maddie smiled at Marsha. "Wow, that's so cool. I mean, I'm no financial expert or anything. Heck, I have no idea what price we're asking. But one thing

I do know is that Dad would be thrilled if it were you who bought the store. He likes you, Marsha. He likes all you guys in his little sales club."

Marsha opened her purse, took out a business card, and handed it to Maddie. "Here, have your broker call me at this number. Don't worry, we'll work out all the details."

Marsha looked around the store. All the shelves were still there, as were the bins full of gardening tools. She also saw the candy machine that Gardener had installed in the back of the store near an electric train set he'd built that ran on three tracks, with all the trimmings. "For the kids," Gardener had said to Marsha, happily manipulating the train's control lever one morning.

The thought of Gardener's leaving and the sale of the store saddened Marsha. But the idea of carrying on his passion—the chance to finally pay him back and pay it forward—had lit a fire in her. "Yep," she thought, "this feels right." She turned back to Maddie. "Well, as long as I'm here, where are the other brooms? I guess we've got some cleaning to do."

Four hours later, after Maddie and Marsha had

cleaned the place from top to bottom, they headed out the door. "Marsha, I really appreciate your hanging around today and cleaning up," Maddie said. "And really, you don't have to feel obligated to buy the store. I'd understand if you changed your mind."

Marsha sighed. The news about Gardener's selling the store had been a blow. But she'd been sent down here today for a reason. "He wants me to buy the store," she thought. "He wants someone with a passion for gardening, like he has, and a passion for sales, like he has, too. He's picking me." That comforted her. "No," she answered, ripping the "For Sale" sign from the door and folding it into her purse. "I won't be changing my mind."

Six months later

Marsha pulled up a chair in her small, cramped office and began tallying the day's receipts. It had been a busy day, with plenty of customers in and out of her store asking questions about harvesting tomatoes, pruning roses, and dealing with depleted soil. Exhausted but happy, she reflected on the past six months. They'd been a blur—the news of Gardener and his store; the purchase of the store (which she continued to call Rawlings Garden Supply); frequent visits from Brenda Cobb, Jake Carson, and the rest of the Saturday Morning Sales Club gang; and her flourishing sales career.

Marsha had also toyed with the decision of retiring and running the store full time. Gardener was against it. "You're still young, and you're still a top producer at your company," he said to Marsha over lunch one day between trips. "You've got a PDA chock-full of happy customers. It's too early to leave yet."

Marsha talked it over with her financial planner, and they decided that even though she'd earned quite a bit of money in recent years, she would continue in her career and devote weekends and the odd holiday to her new garden shop.

Perhaps the best news was that Maddie had agreed to run the store on a full-time basis until she decided what to do with the rest of her life. Marsha had found a friend in Gardener, and now she'd found one in his daughter, too. Her youthful sense of optimism was a tonic for Marsha, who liked having her around for her warmth and friendliness toward the store customers, and also as a fond reminder of Gardener. The apple hadn't fallen too far from the tree, it turned out, and Marsha was glad to keep the Rawlings family connection going at the store.

She greeted the visits from Brenda, Jake, and Ted enthusiastically, as well. The back-and-forth, the kidding and repartee, and especially the warm early memories of Gardener and the Saturday Morning Sales Club provided Marsha a welcome respite from the busy life of a small-business owner. Every Saturday morning a few old friends would show up, and Marsha was glad she was able to keep the Saturday Morning Sales Club going. It was a tradition now, and she knew that Gardener would love it—he'd be laughing at all the antics and high-spirited debates about the sales garden he'd invented.

Thinking about opening her own garden store brought up a special memory. It had been a warm spring day, with a steady flow of customers in and out of the store. Marsha saw a young woman, maybe in her early thirties, listlessly wandering down the aisles looking at the displays. Marsha gave the woman some space, but after a while she noticed that the woman was still halfheartedly checking out some plants. Marsha decided to see if she could help.

"Hi there," she said. "Anything I can do for you?"

The woman sighed softly before answering. "Not unless you can find me a new career," she said ruefully.

Marsha held out her hand. "Hi, I'm Marsha Molloy. I'm the owner."

"Kelly. Kelly Austin," the woman replied, returning Marsha's handshake. "I'm only kind of joking about the career thing. Just hasn't been a good week, I guess."

"Oh?" Marsha said. "What business are you in?" She suspected she knew the answer already.

"I'm in sales—though I'm not selling much these days," Kelly replied.

Marsha thought of Gardener before answering. "Boy, have you come to the right place."

The Sales Garden Model

Planning

🌱 Personal vision
  See it in detail
  Talk about it often

🌱 Set up a support group
  Find positive people
  Structure conversation

Harvesting

🌱 Timing
  "Pick" the produce
  when it's ready
  No forcing the close

🌱 Investing in renewal
  Celebrate the sale
  Show appreciation

Sales Garden

Seeding

🌱 Persistence
  Continuous activity
  Consistent follow-up

🌱 Connected relationships
  Customer's best interest
  first
  Foundation in mutual
  trust and respect

Nurturing

🌱 Conscious caring
  Know your "personal
  best practices"
  Do them often

🌱 Doing the right thing
  Find what is best for
  customers and do it
  Take the extra step

The Sales Garden Glossary

Fertilizer Information or actions the gardener uses to promote the sale

Fun Enjoying the challenge of sales and finding it meaningful

Gardener A salesperson who tends a sales garden

Gardening time A state of mind where one reflects on the present and plans for the future

Good soil A sales territory with good potential

Harvest Closing sales agreements at the right time in a manner that ensures renewal of the customer relationship

Nurturing Taking care of customers and potential customers

Perennials Customers who come back year after year

Planning Creating a personal vision for success and the action steps that support it

Sales garden A metaphor that looks at a sales career in terms of planting, growing, and harvesting

Saturday Morning Sales Club Support group for salespeople

Seeding Any act of contacting new customers and building relationships

Storms Unexpected events that disrupt your sale

Watering Staying connected and supporting customers

Weeds and pests The competition or people who are negative to your sale

$PROUT!

Contact Us!

❧ Greg and Alan would love to hear from you. How are you using the SPROUT! message? What new ideas can you share with other SPROUT! sales gardeners?

❧ Call about the SPROUT! four-hour seminar: create a Sales Garden plan for your group with this interactive half-day workshop that complements any other sales approach. Follow-up learning available one-on-one through sales coaches.

❧ Keynote speeches add high energy and new sales thinking to any group function.

Alan Vengel
Vengel Lash Associates
877-691-8761
vla@vengellash.com
www.VengelLash.com

Greg Wright
C. G. Wright Associates
760-929-1790
www.CGWA.com

About the Authors

Alan Vengel

Alan Vengel is a founding partner of Vengel Lash Associates, Inc. and a strategic partner with Beverly Kaye & Associates/Career Systems International. He is a consultant, speaker, and educator in the subjects of influence, negotiation, sales, and talent development.

In addition to providing training and consulting services to more than three hundred of America's largest corporations, he has been a featured speaker at American Society for Training & Development (ASTD) national conferences and the Linkage Leadership Conference.

Alan has an undergraduate degree from the University of Florida and a master's degree from the University of Arizona. His last book, *The Influence Edge: How to Persuade Others to Help You Achieve Your Goals* (Berrett-Koehler Publishers, 2000), was nominated for a California Book Award.

Greg Wright

Over the past twenty-seven years, Greg Wright has worked with business leaders and sales professionals from some of the best-performing companies in the world. His work on leadership and sales success has been implemented in a range of industries on six continents.

Greg is an Annapolis graduate with an advanced degree from the University of Arkansas. He served during the Vietnam War before starting his training and consulting business, C.G. Wright & Associates (CGWA), in San Diego, California. CGWA continues to provide performance solutions to corporate America.

A Mississippi native, Greg lives in the Florida Keys with his wife. Their garden yields bananas, mangoes, and key limes.

Berrett-Koehler books and audios are available at quantity discounts for orders of 10 or more copies.

SPROUT!
Everything I Need to Know about Sales I Learned from My Garden
4 Steps to Sales Success

Alan Vengel and Greg Wright

Hardcover
ISBN 1-57675-207-0
Item #52070 $19.95

To find out about discounts on orders of 10 or more copies for individuals, corporations, institutions, and organizations, please call us toll-free at (800) 929-2929.

To find out about our discount programs for resellers, please contact our Special Sales department at (415) 288-0260; Fax: (415) 362-2512.
Or email us at bkpub@bkpub.com.

Subscribe to our free e-newsletter!

To find out about what's happening at Berrett-Koehler and to receive announcements of our new books, special offers, free excerpts, and much more, subscribe to our free monthly e-newsletter at **www.bkconnection.com**.

Berrett-Koehler Publishers
PO Box 565, Williston, VT 05495-9900
Call toll-free! **800-929-2929** 7 am-9 pm EST

Or fax your order to 802-864-7627
For fastest service order online: **www.bkconnection.com**